Praise For
Henri Nouwen and Spiritual Polarities: A Life of Tension

"In this last volume of his trilogy on Henri Nouwen, Wil Hernandez offers us a book that will be of value to many more than that already large group of people who have come to appreciate Nouwen's spiritual wisdom. While it offers an important discussion of the tensions of Nouwen's life and the way they provided the soil in which his penetratingly powerful books grew, more importantly it provides a very helpful discussion of the role of these tensions in the spiritual life in general. It is, therefore, a book at least as much about the dynamics of the spiritual journey as it is a book about one man's journey. And, I predict, it is this broader contribution that this book makes that will ultimately be seen to be its most important. It is an excellent book and I heartily recommend it."

—**David G. Benner, PhD,** psychologist, lecturer, and author of *Soulful Spirituality: Becoming Fully Alive and Fully Human*

"Wil Hernandez deftly explores what is perhaps one of the most important elements of true spiritual maturity—the capacity to hold inner tension and paradox. Through the wisdom of Henri Nouwen, Wil offers us an essential contribution to the field of spirituality. I highly recommend his book for anyone seeking to bring their spiritual life to new depths."

—**Christine Valters Paintner, PhD,** director of Abbey of the Arts and author of *The Artist's Rule: Nurturing Your Creative Soul with Monastic Wisdom*

"Wil Hernandez's book is an important addition to the growing corpus of Nouwen studies. Using the concept of tension as an interpretive key, Hernandez takes us into the heart of Nouwen's spirituality. While it makes for an excellent introduction to Nouwen's thought, it will also not disappoint the Nouwen aficionados."

—**Simon Chan**, Trinity Theological College, Singapore

"*Henri Nouwen and Spiritual Polarities: A Life of Tension* is a carefully researched and documented book that describes the life of Nouwen as pictured through his extensive writings. Using the paradoxical pulls and themes present in every human life, Hernandez shows some authentic challenges that shaped the life of Nouwen and how his transparent descriptions of his life journey can encourage and assist others as they address similar issues. Hernandez writes about tensions within the self, in the community, and in one's relationship with God and how Nouwen saw what might be perceived to be oppositional as all part of the call to integration—to "both/and." This work is both informational and inspirational. It offers a significant contribution to the Nouwen materials and is well worth reading on many levels."

—**Jeannette Bakke**, spiritual director, retreat leader, and author of *Holy Invitations: Exploring Spiritual Direction*

"If you are not yet acquainted with Henri Nouwen, here is the best place I know to get a comprehensive overview of his profound understanding of the Christian life. If you are well read in Nouwen, you will find this a stimulating and creative synthesis of his dialectical perspective of the nature of the Christian life in the world. Wil Hernandez has crafted an excellent presentation of Nouwen that, at the same time, sets forth the essence of the Christian life. Those who are neutral toward or resistant to the contemporary aberrations of the Christian life may well find this book providing a whole new understanding of what the Christian life is about. One that challenges their assumptions. Those for whom Christianity has become a dull habit may be awakened to the living reality that has been subverted by religiosity. This book will be a delight to those who are walking the journey with Nouwen; a challenge to those who question the validity of such a journey; and a danger to those who have domesticated the journey to their own liking."

—**M. Robert Mulholland, Jr.,** author of
*Invitation to a Journey: A Road Map for
Spiritual Formation* and *The Deeper Journey:
The Spirituality of Discovering Your True Self*

"Henri Nouwen scholar Wil Hernandez points to Henri's writings to support his psychological, ministerial, and theological theories regarding the social and spiritual ramifications of living the Gospel in today's world. Wil is a teacher and a guide for all of us who wrestle with the challenges and questions of journeying spiritually in a secular society."

—**Sue Mosteller, CSJ,** Henri Nouwen Legacy Trust

"This book is a masterful guide through the vast landscape of Henri Nouwen's thought. After I read Wil's book, I knew I needed to explore Nouwen more carefully, and I knew that in doing so I would keep *Henri Nouwen and Spiritual Polarities* nearby throughout the exploration."

—**Evan B. Howard,** director of Spirituality Shoppe: An Evangelical Center for the Study of Christian Spirituality

"In this third book of his trilogy on Henri Nouwen's spirituality, Wil Hernandez offers a considerable gift to those of us on the journey toward Christian spiritual maturity. Many of us struggle in these postmodern times with the issue of how to be faithful to foundational Christian principles, while also recognizing that we can no longer claim the certainty and simple clarity that sustained us in the past. Hernandez's interpretation of Nouwen's life and writings does not dodge the ambiguity and tension that constitute contemporary life. But his understanding of Nouwen does reveal creative ways to move in and through brokenness, weakness, and suffering into the unfailing embrace of the Beloved. Scripturally based, Hernandez's clarity and humility of voice make *Henri Nouwen and Spiritual Polarities* a compelling read."

—**Norvene Vest,** spiritual director and author of *Re-Visioning Theology*

"Our spiritual journey, a real mixture of contradictions, mystery, compassion, and sometimes chaos, is out of place in a world that prefers order, closure, and tidiness. Henri Nouwen's practice of 'befriending'—life is not 'either-or,' but 'both-and'—is an invitation to embrace our fullness precisely because we invite both sorrow and love, untidiness and beauty, into our exquisitely human world. Wil Hernandez's portrait of Nouwen's life of tension is grace-giving indeed."

—**Terry Hershey,** author of *The Power of Pause: Becoming More by Doing Less*

"Following the structure of his previous books that describes the *inward, outward,* and *upward* journeys of Henri Nouwen, Wil Hernandez now explores the psychological, ministerial, and theological dynamics of his tension-filled life and why we resonate with it. Applying Richard Rohr's insight of 'nondualistic consciousness,' he offers a compelling portrait, not only of Henri's tension-filled life, but also of the inner terrain of nearly everyone who attempts to resolve the complexities, contradictions, and polarities of their spiritual experience. Henri's gift is authentic articulation of the struggle in the journey toward wholeness; Hernandez's contribution is in helping us name the polarity, and consciously and creatively deal with tensions within the paradoxes in the human psyche."

—**Michael J. Christensen, PhD,** associate professor of spirituality, Drew University, and co-editor of *Spiritual Formation: Following the Movements of the Spirit* by Henri Nouwen

"Wil Hernandez's third book focusing on spiritual polarities in a life of tension is well-written and helpful, containing many gems of spiritual wisdom. I highly recommend it as essential reading for a fuller understanding of Henri Nouwen, and a deeper spiritual life in Christ."
—**Rev. Siang-Yang Tan, PhD**, professor of psychology, Fuller Theological Seminary, and senior pastor, First Evangelical Church Glendale in Southern California

"Wil Hernandez provides us with transforming and challenging insights drawn from the wonderful writings of Henri Nouwen. In this final installment of his trilogy, Wil uses Nouwen's words to challenge our tendency toward either/or thinking and invites us to journey into the profound, perplexing, and freeing world of both/and thinking, a world of tension, paradox, and mystery—a world Nouwen called home. Wil masterfully weaves Nouwen's words into a tapestry that clearly and insightfully conveys the intricacies and complexities involved in both/and thinking and its ramifications for the living of life and the doing of ministry."
—**Larry Warner**, author of *Journey with Jesus*

"This reflective and insightful book studies a man whose life tensions presented themselves as challenges with which we can identify, and invitations to depth and conversion we can hope to emulate. This work will help all ministers and those who support them on the journey inward, outward, and Godward."
—**Michael Horan, PhD**, professor and chair of Theological Studies, Loyola Marymount University

"Wil Hernandez has a knack for summarizing Nouwen's prolific writings without draining the life out of them. Wil also has the ability to select just the right Nouwen quote so that this man's amazing witness may speak once more to our increasingly polarized and alienated world. What an important figure Nouwen is today, and what a great service Hernandez provides in writing this book!"
—**Jerry P. Haas**, spiritual director, Upper Room Ministries

"Wil Hernandez has already established himself as one of the leading interpreters of Henri Nouwen's work. With this, the final book in his triology on Nouwen, Wil integrates the tensive polarities that existed in Nouwen's life and work, and indeed, the tensive polarities that make up the fabric of authentic Christian spirituality. A must read for Nouwen enthusiasts and those seeking wholeness in our fragmented, dualistic world."

—**Kenneth W. Brewer, PhD,** chair, Department of Theology at Spring Arbor University

Henri Nouwen and Spiritual Polarities

Henri Nouwen and Spiritual Polarities

A LIFE OF TENSION

Wil Hernandez

PAULIST PRESS
New York / Mahwah, NJ

Cover photograph by Frank Hamilton. Used with permission.
Cover design by Joel B. Dasalla
Interior artwork by Jason Chen. Used with permission.
Book design by Lynn Else

Library of Congress Cataloging-in-Publication Data

Hernandez, Wil.
    Henri Nouwen and spiritual polarities : a life of tension / Wil Hernandez.
      pages cm
    Includes bibliographical references and index.
    ISBN 978-0-8091-4741-0 (alk. paper) — ISBN 978-1-61643-137-2
  1. Nouwen, Henri J. M. 2. Polarity—Religious aspects—Christianity. 3. Spiritual life—Christianity. 4. Christianity. I. Title.
    BX4705.N87H48 2012
    282.092—dc23

                                 2011047674

Published by Paulist Press
997 Macarthur Boulevard
Mahwah, New Jersey 07430

www.paulistpress.com

Printed and bound in the
United States of America

To
Dr. Richard Peace
my longtime mentor and greatest advocate
at Fuller Seminary
who has always believed the best in me
and continues to do so, no matter what

Contents

CONTENTS

Foreword

Every so often—in fact, not infrequently—people come into the world who are seers for the rest of us. Henri Nouwen was surely such a person, and this study by Wil Hernandez is helping us not just to see this excellent seer, but to invite us into the same seeing.

I knew Henri personally in his intermediate years both through personal sharings, written correspondence (which I can no longer find), joining him on retreats, and one more extended visit when he came to observe our life at the New Jerusalem lay community in Cincinnati in the late 1970s. He was a complex man who nevertheless saw with a great and clear simplicity for the rest of us.

Henri surely must have paid the price within himself for this transmutation of message from complex to simple. As St. Paul says of himself, "Death is at work in us, but life in you" (2 Cor 4:12). If I am to be honest, I envied him in his ability to write with such utter luminosity about profound spiritual things. It was like he had two different levels to his being, and we were all the beneficiaries of the brighter level. He suffered the darker level himself, but turned that into gift and blessing. Maybe there is no other way?

He wrote me once in the mid 1980s when I was first establishing the Center for Action and Contemplation in New Mexico. He congratulated me on the name of the center, and then in several letters encouraged me to consider teaching "nothing else" except this contemplative mind and heart that both the world and the church needed so much. "Don't let anything else get in the way!" he said. He knew, and I am more convinced now myself, that contemplation is indeed the *change that changes everything*. It was that level of seeing that bore so much fruit in him for the rest of us, and made his writing so clean and clear, even when English was not his native language.

He wrote me once that he had discovered the wisdom of several Eastern teachers, and particularly recommended Eknath Easwaran for my study and consideration. I mention this here because it reveals an interesting aspect to his brilliant personality. Henri knew that his message was essential and important for Western Christianity, and he would avoid anything that was too controversial—lest it be used to avoid what he knew *he had to say, should say, and wanted to say*. He followed his own advice to me, "Don't let anything else get in the way!"

Things like Eastern religions, divisive church issues, social justice issues, moral issues, and sexual issues that separated groups and people were usually left in the background so that the foreground could be made quite clear and compelling. I think it was probably a very wise intuition on his part. We invariably agreed on most of these same concerns, but he was savvy enough to let them influence and form him indirectly, without usually addressing them directly. He knew the politics of religion and the excuses that the ego would use to dismiss the essential Gospel. For me, Henri intuitively lived the advice of Jesus to be "wise as a serpent and innocent as a dove" (Matt 10:16).

Henri made sure that the sterling God questions and essential heart questions, God answers and heart answers, would be and must be absolutely up front and clear; and then trusted that people would have the inner transformation to look at the more divisive issues in a healthy, Gospel, and "nondualistic" way. He was not a crusader, except for the love of God.

Believe me, he was very clear privately about his appreciation for other world religions, the needed reform of the Catholic Church, the needs of the poor and the marginalized, and the lack of even basic spirituality among so many who attend weekly church services. He did not take public sides where sides did not need to be taken—at that time—concerning testy church issues like mandatory celibacy, women priests, rights for homosexuals, liturgical concerns, clericalism, the Papacy, etc. Some might say he lacked courage, and maybe he did; but I would say he knew what was his to do and what was not his to do. Can God, or any of us, ask any more of anybody? That clarity of both vocation and vocabulary kept Henri Nouwen always and invariably "on message"!

I admire and trust Wil Hernandez's framing of Nouwen's thought in terms of his natural ability to be a nondualistic thinker, and his ability to hold would-be tensions in a very creative balance. I think it was this passion that drew us to one another. He lived and loved paradox, and knew there was a new wisdom to be had if we held both sides of difficult questions face to face. He invariably made both faces shine with a new brilliance.

I thank Wil Hernandez for continuing to study and disseminate the brilliant gifts and Gospel-centered ministry of Henri Nouwen. This book, and his two other previous studies on Nouwen, are now keeping us all *on message!* Wil has become a friend of a friend, who was an inspired friend to all who love the simple and wondrous Gospel of Life. His writings and his ministry will stand the tests of time, because Henri Nouwen saw and wrote from a bright and clear level that is always true.

Richard Rohr, OFM
Center for Action and Contemplation
Albuquerque, New Mexico

Preface

After teaching many courses on the spirituality of Henri Nouwen and leading numerous seminars, workshops, and retreats all across the country based on his works for over six years, I have become ever more aware of a recurring theme around the dynamics of tension in his journey. I have touched on this subject previously in my two books—*Henri Nouwen: A Spirituality of Imperfection* (2006)[1] and *Henri Nouwen and Soul Care: A Ministry of Integration* (2008)[2]—although in a more broad-sweep fashion.

One event that brought this issue back to my attention was a workshop I attended in 2007 at the Los Angeles Religious Education Congress conducted by Fr. Richard Rohr, OFM, on the intriguing subject of nondualistic thinking—a "both-and" way of thinking directly related to the capacity to integrate opposites versus splitting them off. [3] While listening to Rohr speak about Jesus as the supreme example of such a mindset, I remember saying to myself that Henri Nouwen not only subscribed to such a manner of thinking, he lived it throughout his journey; Nouwen exemplified a nondualistic lifestyle.

Some three years after that workshop, Rohr published a much more exhaustive treatment of his initial talk in book form, entitled *The Naked Now: Learning to See as the Mystics See.*[4] I picked up a copy right away and devoured it as if it were an entirely new subject to me. The book delivered far more than what I had expected from it.

So affected was I, that I found myself one day sitting in a Chinese restaurant, barely concentrating on eating my favorite shrimp fried rice and instead feverishly scribbling down one idea after another that was flowing rapidly through my mind—mainly about how Rohr's writing rang so true for Henri Nouwen's journeying experience. By the time I finally got done with my lunch, I not only had a conceptual outline etched in my head; much to my satisfaction, I also ended up identifying most of the chapter headings and section titles. I left the restaurant that day with overflowing excitement at the prospect of a new book proposal.

A few more months passed by, however, before I could solidify my initial idea. It took another Rohr talk, based on his then-newly released book at the 2010 Los Angeles Religious Education Congress, to push me to start actually writing the current material. I now see this work as a fitting way to round off a trilogy—consistent with Nouwen's now-famous flair for employing a three-point format in many of his writings—with the body of work originating from my PhD dissertation on Henri Nouwen.

The basic content of this book, therefore, emerged directly out of my dissertation, now dating back more than seven years. However, it was Rohr's more recent work that brought the seed back to life. His articulation of nondualism prompted me to look back and reexamine more closely Henri Nouwen's abundant application of it in his own journey. In short, I owe much of the inspiration for this new book to Richard Rohr. I am therefore delightfully favored that he has written the Foreword.

The Main Focus of This Book

To issue a claim that Henri Nouwen espoused a nondualistic consciousness in the way he lived out his spirituality and journey is to underscore the fact that he possessed an innate capacity to see life not in strictly black *or* white, but in a black *and* white; thus he was able to function in a gray zone, revealing his nuanced creative skill. One of his former coworkers at L'Arche Daybreak said this about him: "Henri's life and writings witnessed that reflective human lives will be big, varied, and often full of contradictions. Throughout his life Henri had an affinity with a complex, multifaceted orientation to life."[5] He was not drawn to the inflexible, tightly controlled way of handling life to which dualists usually succumb.

Indeed, Nouwen, for the most part, confronted all manner of contradictions—real and imagined—head-on without splitting them off, but rather with a conscious intent to integrate them into his personal experience. He had an instinctive knack for being able to "befriend" the existing polarities of life. In short, Nouwen well understood that all of life incorporates tension. He learned both the art and the process of living creatively in and through this reality, with a mixture of struggle and success.

This book is about the tension-filled journey of Henri Nouwen, and centers around his inward, outward, and upward (or Godward) resolve to live out the dialectical tensions that characterize much of spiritual life. Nouwen embodied the contemplative lifestyle of a true mystic who was able to see through spiritual realities—above, beyond, beneath, and underneath the surface of things. Anyone familiar with his writings—his journals in particular—cannot fail to be struck by his uncanny ability to perceive one piece of reality in terms of its correlation to the other pieces. For him, all of life was interconnected in some mystical way. Nouwen's entire existence, though by all measures far from perfect, seemed always to be heading and gravitating toward fuller, higher, wider, and deeper aspects of integration. His constant movement in this direction appeared effortless and unforced.

Moreover, Henri Nouwen devoted his life to following Jesus' way—which was "the way of love but also the way of suffering" (*RO*:149)—what Rohr refers to as the "two universal and prime paths of transformation."[6] Indeed, as poignantly depicted in many of his writings, Nouwen loved much and suffered much all throughout his lifetime. Love and suffering were anything but strange bedfellows in his experience.

Much can be said about the aphorism that the one who loves much suffers much. For to surrender to love is akin to risking, to letting go of one's proclivity to control, thereby opening oneself to vulnerable living, and consequently inviting the real prospect of suffering. It is equally accurate to say that only one who has known the experience of deep suffering can freely love and give love with true abandon. If suffering happens to be the consequence of true love, then that same love also becomes the fruit of real suffering. Nouwen, from his own experience, reminds you and me: "Yes, as you love deeply the ground of your heart will be broken more and more, but you will rejoice in the abundance of the fruit it will bear" (*IVL*:60).

Henri Nouwen loved lavishly and in so doing suffered immensely. But his journey attests to the fact that it was his deep immersion in a life of suffering that fueled his ever-growing capacity to love—himself, others, and God. Indeed, love and suffering are bound to change anyone radically. Nouwen believed they both deepen and expand the quality of our hearts (*IVL:59*).

It is safe to conclude that the twin dynamics of love and suffering were the main contributing factors to Henri Nouwen's personal wholeness and integration. For according to Rohr, love and suffering open up our life space, leading to a more unified field of experience, which is the integrated field.[7] This might well have been what enabled Nouwen to openly welcome and embrace a life of ongoing tension.

My Approach to This Work

The primary method employed in this work is decidedly that of data synthesis via a combination of descriptive-interpretive analysis similar to the two previous books I have written on Henri Nouwen. Thus, every assertion I make here comes out of my own interpretive analyses of Nouwen's works, which are only limited by the available sources I have chosen to access.

I did not have the fortune of encountering Nouwen personally. I wish I had. Yet never once have I felt deprived or disadvantaged because of that. After years of intensive study of Henri Nouwen's voluminous writings, reinforced by ongoing interactions with various thoughtful students and highly educated retreatants over the years, I would like to believe that my reading of Nouwen has broadened and sharpened to a considerable degree. In saying this I do not wish to imply that the conclusions I have arrived at about Nouwen are infallible.

What I genuinely hope is that my sense of objectivity concerning my subject matter has been sharpened substantially. Through the years I have been forced to more humbly engage in a constant rereading of Henri Nouwen's texts, aided by other avid readers' serious engagement and critical reassessments of his views and positions. I have likewise been periodically challenged by others about my own interpretations, which I would never dare claim to be one hundred percent accurate.

Nobody is able to completely capture who Nouwen was in all of his complexity, not even those knew him personally. Yet interestingly, I once had an encounter with a retreatant who had known Nouwen in a certain relational capacity, and who flatly refused to accept any other view than the one he staunchly held about the person of Nouwen.

The truth is, many people have experienced Henri Nouwen in a variety of different ways and contexts, which at times seem contradictory. A case in point is when I conducted a series of interviews in 2003 and 2004 with people who knew Nouwen well. One set of interviewees portrayed Nouwen as a quintessentially absentminded professor who possessed a scattered brain, unable to fully focus, and exhibiting boundless energy that would be normative for someone suffering from adult ADD. Conversely, I encountered some folks who swore that Nouwen was one of the most centered individuals that you could possibly meet on planet Earth, and that when you were with him, he could make you feel like you were the only person in the entire universe. So the question is: Who was the real Henri Nouwen based on these two opposing points of view?

Could it be that both camps are equally right in their differing perceptions of Nouwen, based on their direct, albeit limited, experience of him? The same can be said for those who feel certain that they can pin down Nouwen's temperament with precision—either as an extrovert or an introvert. What if he was both? Donald McNeill, a former colleague of his at the University of Notre Dame, was right. Henri Nouwen simply did not fit our oftentimes rigid categorizations. His unique personality defies such attempts to pigeonhole him.[8]

That said, I wish to state clearly—at the risk of sounding apologetic—that my own limited attempt to interpret one facet of the dynamics of Henri Nouwen's journey is to be construed as neither the only nor the most comprehensive interpretation of it. Nonetheless, a thorough synthesis of his writings reveals a pattern that warrants careful consideration on the part of every serious student of Nouwen. His spiritual journey is, by all means, discernible if one pays attention to his integrated manner of thinking.

Although it would have been such a delightful treat, it really is not absolutely necessary to have met Nouwen in person to be able to arrive at some reasonably established conclusions about his thinking processes. Thankfully, Henri Nouwen was so unapologetically transparent in all his writings that his readers can easily access and know him well. That in itself is a precious gift that Nouwen gave to us all. He genuinely longed to be known for the true person that he was. Thus, from what we can glean from him through his writings, we stand to learn much from his example—from both his inherent strengths and his limitations.

The Composition of This Book

This book follows the same basic structure as my two previous works, and it flows out of the foundational constructs laid out in both of them. Therefore, I consider this the final volume in a trilogy treatment of Henri Nouwen's spiritual journey.

The first book, *Henri Nouwen: A Spirituality of Imperfection*, is a broad sketch of Nouwen's journey, divided into two parts, covering the *integrated* and the *imperfect* nature of his journey. Part I introduces the threefold thrust of his journey: the *inward* via solitude, the *outward* via service, and the *upward* via prayer, corresponding to the threefold emphases on *psychology, ministry,* and *theology,* as each of these intertwines with spirituality. Part II underscores the coexistent reality of imperfection in Nouwen's journey by focusing in on its psychological (wholeness through brokenness), ministerial (power through weakness), and theological (communion through suffering) dimensions.

The second book, *Henri Nouwen and Soul Care: A Ministry of Integration*, is a companion to the first and highlights Nouwen's integrated ministry as it emerged out of his equally integrated, albeit imperfect, spirituality. The main focus is on the integrated outworking of his spiritual ministry, which also focuses on the psychological, ministerial, and theological dynamics of his soul care and spiritual companioning approach.

While I address the idea of tension in Henri Nouwen's journey briefly in the previous two books, I expound upon it here more systematically and comprehensively. (As I have already alluded, the theme of tension is organized in a way that is in conjunction with the already familiar structure of the two earlier works—which, in this case, revolves around the dynamics of living with the reality of *psychological, ministerial,* and *theological* tensions in direct correlation with the inward, outward, and upward dialectics of Henri Nouwen's journey.)

Thus, this work naturally falls into three major parts with three chapters in each, featuring a carefully selected pair of spiritual polarities per chapter. I made these choices based on an abundance of sources, and I must admit it was not easy to decide which pairs to include in the final line-up; there were certainly other variables to consider. However, I was sure that I wanted to retain the threefold structure that Henri Nouwen has become known for.

An added feature in this book is the inclusion of a set of guide questions for personal reflection at the end of each chapter, followed by a suggested reflective exercise the reader can optionally undertake. Both are designed to translate the body of information in every section into a more personal, experiential, and practical level—allowing the self to "descend with the mind into the heart" (to use Henri Nouwen's oft-quoted phrase of Theophan the Recluse [see *RO*:145]). I am indebted to my friends Annette Kakimoto and Rick Oxenham, whose ideas for this particular segment prove to be both insightful and creative.

Insofar as the documentation of my primary sources on Henri Nouwen is concerned, I utilize the same parenthetical citation here of his works within the text as I did in my first two books. It consists of coded initials of Nouwen's book title followed by page reference(s). For instance, (*RO*:12) refers to *Reaching Out: The Three Movements of the Spiritual Life*, page 12. The reader can refer to pages xxxi–xxxii, which contain the abbreviated title initials arranged alphabetically under the heading "Henri J. M. Nouwen's Cited Works."

Acknowledgments

I suspect I am no different from most authors. I write best when I am away from home—away from my familiar surroundings, which always threaten to derail even my most relentless attempts to concentrate. My preferred venue has always been a retreat center where I could focus the most. Except for my preliminary readings and research, which took place mostly in my private office in Pasadena, California, the greatest portion of the actual writing has come to fruition in various retreat settings across the country.

How often I wished I could just take off for a straight month or two and engage in an uninterrupted writing spree! But, like most people, I did not have that luxury. Instead, I had to find a way, on a number of different occasions, to write while doing my teaching job. I was fortunate to do just that during most of the summer and early fall of 2010. I am so grateful for all the timely invitations and generous accommodations of longtime as well as newfound friends. To these gracious folks, I am deeply indebted!

Many thanks for the hospitality and availability of my two Episcopal friends in San Francisco, Won-Jae Hur and Daniel London, who made it possible for me to spend a week of silence during the first part of June in an ideal location: the New Camaldoli Hermitage, nestled in the rugged coastal mountains of Big Sur, directly overlooking the Pacific Ocean. There I was able to finish most of the first part of the manuscript while experiencing firsthand the typical Benedictine hospitality of the Camaldolese monks.

I continued my writing during the last two weeks of June at the Oblate Renewal Center in San Antonio, Texas, where I also taught a summer intensive course on Henri Nouwen every night at the Oblate School of Theology. I am grateful to the school's president, Fr. Ron Rolheiser, OMI, for the opportunity to teach and write at the same time while residing at their beautiful campus.

Thanks too to Anne Luther of the Institute for Adult Spiritual Renewal for affording me the chance to teach major portions of this material to twenty-five enthusiastic students at the Lakeshore Campus of Loyola Chicago for one week in July. I truly appreciate the wonderful students who offered me invaluable feedback on the subject matter. It was heartwarming to see their eagerness to actively engage in the "field testing" of this new material in my class with them.

My gratitude also goes to Sherry Elliott, the tireless architect of the SOULFeast Conference hosted by the Upper Room Ministries, for inviting me to conduct a series of Nouwen workshops during their July conference at the breathtaking Lake Junaluska Retreat and Conference Center in Asheville, North Carolina. Two of the afternoon seminars specifically addressed the topic of Nouwen's tension-filled journey. The very positive feedback I got from the participants spurred my writing on and helped me bring it to the finish.

For the final week of July, I flew to Long Island, New York, where my nephew Marvin and his wife Julie reside, and spent a week of directed retreat at the gorgeous St. Ignatius Jesuit Retreat House (*Inisfada*) in Manhasset. While receiving valuable guidance from a wise spiritual director (thank you, Sr. Ellen Collesano, RSCJ!) and savoring the beauty and stillness of the place during my weeklong stay, I was inspired to carve out some intentional writing time on the side. My stay there proved to be not only spiritually nourishing, but fruitful for my writing project as well.

For an entire second week in August, I was in the company of several Christian spirituality scholars meeting at St. John's Abbey, Collegeville, Minnesota, where I was able to present a general overview and outline of my book project and receive encouraging feedback from the conference participants (Jim Wilhoit, Tom Schwanda, Klaus Issler, Keith Meyer, and Mike Glerup). In particular, I wish to thank Evan Howard, the founder of Spirituality Shoppe: An Evangelical Center for the Study of Christian Spirituality, for inviting me to be part of this supportive group of mostly academic leaders, who meet annually for fellowship, consultation, and peer review, and are dedicated to promoting and cultivating the field of evangelical spirituality.

ACKNOWLEDGMENTS

While conducting a weekend Nouwen retreat in early September at the Benedictine monastery in Pecos, New Mexico, I took advantage of extending my stay for another week of continued focused writing. I appreciate Br. Jim Marron for paving the way for me to do this in such a conducive monastery setting.

Toward the latter part of September 2010, I finished half of the preliminary draft of this manuscript at the same place where I had worked on my dissertation in 2004—Saint Andrew's Benedictine Abbey in Valyermo, California. Once again, I am profusely thankful to the abbey folks for warmly welcoming me there, most especially Cheryl Evanson, who arranged for my weeklong accommodation. It was such a fruitful stay!

Finally, with a determined spirit and the generous outpouring of prayer support from close friends, I managed to finish the entire manuscript on New Year's Day of 2011. Thank God!

Henri J. M. Nouwen's Cited Works

(Abbreviated Title Initials in Alphabetical List)

LS   *Lifesigns: Intimacy, Fecundity, and Ecstasy in Christian Perspective*

OH   *With Open Hands*

OS   *Out of Solitude*

RO   *Reaching Out: The Three Movements of the Spiritual Life*

RPS   *The Return of the Prodigal Son: A Story of Homecoming*

SD   *Spiritual Direction: Wisdom for the Long Walk of Faith*

SF   *Spiritual Formation: Following the Movements of the Spirit*

WH   *The Wounded Healer: Ministry in Contemporary Society*

WJ   *Walk with Jesus: Stations of the Cross*

WOH *The Way of the Heart: Desert Spirituality and Contemporary Ministry*

Introduction

A Tension-Filled Life

All of creation—animate and inanimate—follows certain rhythmic patterns that are recognizable not only to poets and artists, but to practically anybody who takes the time to reflect and notice them. Just as the ocean tides ebb and flow, so does life. As the sun rises and sets, life too comes and goes. Nowhere is the reality of life's rhythms unfolded more intriguingly than in the highly complex but sacred process of our own journey.

In a spiritual sense, the sacrality of our journey is made more evident by the manifestation of the Divine Presence "in whom we live, and move, and have our being" (Acts 17:28). Such presence—however expressed—is embodied in the mysterious character of our spiritual journey. God is Mystery, and the very nature of mystery breeds tension. Our finite minds can only comprehend so much of spiritual reality, and therefore it behooves us to learn to live with a certain measure of ambiguity and tension. For mystery is indeed "pregnant with hundreds of levels of unfolding and realization."[1]

In singling out, for instance, the mystery that is God, how can we even begin to fathom the fact that God is portrayed in Scripture as both transcendent and immanent, hidden and revealed, unknowable and knowable, unreachable and accessible, universal and local? And how is it that sometimes God seems absent while at other times God appears very present to us? Or, as one of Henri Nouwen's interpreters describes it, "with God, we seem to experience both an intimate union and estrangement all in one breath."[2] At best, we can only *attempt* to explain God, in much the same way that we can only try to make sense of certain realities in our lives in rather limited ways. Nouwen himself reminds us, "God cannot be 'caught' or 'comprehended' in any

---

specific idea, concept, opinion, or conviction" (*SF:4*). There simply is no way we can even contain God in our minds.

If our mysterious God has deliberately chosen to communicate with us at times via the enigmatic means of antinomies, paradoxes, and polarities, then it should not surprise us to find ourselves wrestling with them amidst the realities of our own journeying experience. Tension inevitably accompanies life's inviolate rhythms—whether they pertain to light and darkness, joy and sorrow, or life and death. Our entire journey is filled with tension, from which there is no escaping.

The Nature of Spiritual Tension

In general, tension arises when we face various elements of irony, anomaly, absurdity, opposition, or contradiction in our experience. Our minds are baffled just as our hearts are upset when things seem not to make sense. We demand inner resolution, only to have to admit to ourselves that we may never really find it in our lifetime.

Henri Nouwen confronted the reality of spiritual tension with a tinge of resignation through an honest question, coupled with an equally honest confession: "Can the tension be resolved in an integrated life?...I certainly have not" (*SJ:39*). Implied in Nouwen's answer is the utter reality that in this life, tension is irresolvable. Perhaps it is never meant to be solved. Our experience of it is not bound to subside. It is what it is! But we can, by all means, hold it creatively and let tension result in our own growth.

Many of the spiritual tensions we encounter are primarily situated within the realms of *paradox, antinomy,* or *polarity*. At times, we face some combination of all three. There are abundant examples of each of these in virtually all of Henri Nouwen's writings. It almost seems as though Nouwen thrived in such a tensional environment, welcoming various facets of tension as he would familiar friends.

PARADOX

To give a basic definition, a *paradox* is characterized by a self-contradictory proposition that can appear absurd or nonsensical. The absurdity is embedded in the rhetoric. In describing certain paradoxes of Christian experience, Paul uses this type of play on words in his letter to the Corinthians: "as unknown, and yet are well known; as dying, and see—we are alive; as punished, and yet not killed; as sorrowful, yet always rejoicing; as poor, yet making many rich; as having nothing, and yet possessing everything" (2 Cor 6:9–10).

Like Thomas Merton, who was fond of dialectics, Henri Nouwen was much at home with paradox. Not only did he employ it to brilliant effect in his works; he lived with it well in his own life, in that he was always caught up in a "web of paradoxes" (GD:14). Paradox permeated his life, his actions, and, most especially, his words. Listen to Nouwen's tone, which is quite reminiscent of Paul's words above:

> There is so much darkness to be dispelled, so much deceit to be unmasked, and so many ambitions to be resolved...I am still waiting, yet already receiving; still hoping, yet already possessing; still wondering, yet already knowing. (IM:61–62)

Interestingly, Henri Nouwen's savvy play on words celebrates postmodern culture's emerging new wisdom—"one centered in paradox and contradiction."[3]

ANTINOMY

Another source of spiritual tension that we confront all the time, especially in Scriptures, is called *antinomy*, which is often confused with paradox. As in paradox, the same element of contradiction is present, except that the appearance of contradiction does not reside in the clever phrasing of the language, but rather, is constituted in the very nature of the propositions being articulated. In an antinomy, both sides are substantiated by factual evidence, making the arguments for each side equally tenable despite their seeming lack of reconciliation.[4] For this reason, one is compelled to accept both positions as legitimate.

Take, for example, the fact that Scriptures speak of divine sovereignty side by side with human responsibility. How can both be true at the same time? But somehow they are. In a fascinating way, Paul exemplifies a specific outworking of an antinomy when he urges the Philippians (Phil 2:13) to "work out their salvation with fear and trembling" (as a critical mandate of their human responsibility), while quickly adding: "for it is God who is at work both to will and to work for his good pleasure" (in direct reference to God's sovereignty). Here we have a statement formulated within a single verse of Scripture, which contains two apparently contradictory ideas that are both conveyed to be spiritually true.

POLARITY

What about *polarity?* Polarity, at its simplest, refers to the presence of two opposites. When two contrasting principles are placed side-by-side or invoked simultaneously, tension predictably rises. Most of us are trained to think dualistically, and we bristle at the thought that two opposites can be accommodated together. Our natural instincts tell us that polar opposites ought to be separated and distinguished, since they are, after all, "opposed" to each other. We are unable, or worse, we refuse, to grasp their possible coexistence.

Our main difficulty, as Richard Rohr reveals, lies in the human mind's propensity to operate in binary terms, using comparison, which has a self-canceling effect, consequently producing false dichotomies.[5] It requires a massive reframing of our minds to deal creatively with the tension that polarity stirs up in us.

For Henri Nouwen, this meant learning to embrace and befriend spiritual polarities. Of the three types of tension we have just discussed, Henri Nouwen seemed most drawn to polarities—whether they be inner or outer in nature—as his writings consistently show.

Spiritual Polarities

In his master's thesis, Preston Busch theorizes that Nouwen must have internalized certain key patterns of conceptual resolution in order to cushion the inherent tension involved in his pursuit of integration for himself. Busch classifies polarity into two types of movements, "conversional" and "cooperative":

With conversional polarity the maturing movement is away from a less mature, and toward a more mature pole...[With] cooperative…the maturing movement is between the two poles that cooperate with rather than compete against each other.[6]

Busch gives an example of conversional movement as "light at one end of the continuum and darkness on the other end, the maturing movement being from darkness into light."[7] This is exactly what Robert Jonas refers to as "Henri-ism," which frames "the spiritual life as a journey from *this* to *that*,"[8] similar to Michael Christensen and Rebecca Laird's "inner polarities" in their co-edited book, *Spiritual Formation: Following the Movements of the Spirit* (SF:xxv).

Nowhere is this type of movement more lucidly illustrated than in Nouwen's book, *Reaching Out: The Three Movements of the Spiritual Life*. Here Nouwen stresses our need to "convert" loneliness to solitude, hostility to hospitality, and illusion to prayer (RO:18). Clearly, the movements are progressional.

With "cooperative polarity," Busch engages the concept of breathing to highlight the back and forth movement between two poles. As he further explains, "breathing in and breathing out would be at opposite ends of a continuum, and yet as a person inhales and then exhales, they cooperate to sustain life and allow growth."[9]

Busch's two-pronged conception of polarity is validated in many of Henri Nouwen's writings. Our primary emphasis in this book will be on the "cooperative" strand. In this regard, we often find Nouwen assembling two polar opposites and establishing a case for making both of them "cooperate" amidst the inherent tension of either their alternating or overlapping movements.

Appealing to psychologist James Hillman's popular use of the term "befriending," Henri Nouwen chose this way to describe the dynamic process involved in navigating our way through the tension triggered by spiritual polarities (see LC:29–30). Nouwen showed a high level of tolerance for regarding polar opposites not necessarily as conceptual "enemies" to be pitted against each other, but rather as "friends" that could complement each other.

INTEGRATION AND IMPERFECTION

A classic illustration of how Henri Nouwen managed to contain two polarities side by side in his experience is documented in my first book *Henri Nouwen: A Spirituality of Imperfection.* Here we find the unique substance of Nouwen's counterintuitive journey—a journey toward integration simultaneous with a journey of imperfection—epitomized.

> Henri Nouwen's proclivity for integration represented a major step toward wholeness. On a much deeper analysis, his commitment to pursuing integrity spoke more about his heightened awareness of his fractured human condition than an obsessive drive for perfection. Nouwen's integrative pursuit of the spiritual life never obviated but instead incorporated facets of psychological, ministerial, and theological imperfections. For Nouwen, integration coexisted with the glaring realities of imperfection.[10]

Whereas many of us would not normally conceive of the concept of integration alongside the idea of imperfection, Nouwen regarded both constructs as working hand-in-hand. In his view, one could advance toward perfection through imperfection. We are in fact "perfected" in the process as we attend openly and with integrity to our imperfect but redeemable condition.

Henri Nouwen welcomed the simultaneous outworking of brokenness and healing, power and powerlessness, glory and suffering as conjoined realities in our journey. The road to perfect completion runs through our incomplete integration.

In summary, our route to psychological wholeness entails a massive confrontation with our state of brokenness; ministerially speaking, power can only be perfected via the place of weakness; theologically, the process of our union with God is, of necessity, paved by suffering. What may appear contradictory at first glance, Nouwen reckoned as normative expressions of our life with God; he embraced them as givens. However, that is not to say that Nouwen accepted such realities without a fight. His writings reveal that he struggled all the way through. And although he struggled, he never broke down completely; he always managed to bounce back. Nouwen lived with and through the inward, outward, and upward tensions of his own journey.

In the following three sections, I will endeavor to examine closely each of these three dimensions: the *inward, outward,* and *upward* tensions—and their corresponding *psychological, ministerial,* and *theological* dynamics. For each dimension, I feature three sets of carefully selected spiritual polarities. The aim is to identify the nature and the basic sources of these tensions, together with their dynamic outworking in our lives. Ultimately, the thrust here is for us to learn from Henri Nouwen's own examples how we too can creatively deal with a life of tension in a way that stimulates a deeper experience of transformation in our journey.

PART I

Living with *Inward* Polarities
(Psychological Tensions)

The first and most basic task of the one who takes the inward journey of the heart is to clarify the immense confusion that can arise when people enter into this new internal world.

Henri Nouwen, Spiritual Formation

CHAPTER ONE

True Self and False Self

Solitude is the place of the great struggle and the great encounter—the struggle against the compulsion of the false self, and the encounter with the loving God who offers himself as the substance of the new self.

Henri Nouwen, *The Way of the Heart*

All throughout his life, Henri Nouwen embarked on an interior journey to his deepest self—the place he believed to be his "first source of search and research" (*RO*:29). Like Thomas Merton, one of his heroes in the faith, he made it a point to make sense of his inward life, focusing primarily on the experience of the self that, despite its being "weak" and "false," had inherent authenticity that is rooted in mystery—"a sense of self able to transcend itself and to be in communion with others and with God."[1]

Nouwen well understood this authentic self's capacity for transcendence, which is grounded in the mystical reality of the divine spark alive in each and every human being who is fashioned in the very image of God. This *imago Dei* in us is what has given birth to our true self, constituting our original identity in God. Indeed, "God has sowed his image...the seed of the divine nature" in us all, as the Dominican mystic Meister Eckhart pointed out.[2] Sadly, as we now are only painfully aware, this "original blessing" that marks our core identity has been corrupted by the invasion of the "original sin," rendering us powerless to mirror the glory of God we once fully possessed but now have utterly fallen short of (Rom 3:23).

As a further consequence, the marring of our true self has given way to the elaborate construction of our many false selves. Thus, many of us today live lives far removed from who we originally were meant to be, woefully disconnected from our deepest self. Not only have we become thoroughly oblivious to our real identity, we have slid into such confusion that we could not tell who we truly are anymore. As Nouwen lamented, it is from this "hidden center" that "we are most alienated from ourselves... strangers in our own house" (LM:74).

How then can we recover from this so-called "fall from glory" and thus be enabled to reclaim our original position in God? Providentially, in God's redemptive act in and through the person of Christ, we can, by faith, acquire a "new self" that can empower us to come back home to our true, original self. The apostle Paul dramatically portrays this process for us: "And all of us, with unveiled faces, seeing the glory of the Lord as though reflected in a mirror, are being transformed into the same image from one degree of glory to another" (2 Cor 3:18). Echoing a generally familiar Eastern Orthodox language, Nouwen paraphrases the same verse this way: As we "imagine the reality of the divine as fully as possible...we can slowly be divinized by that reality" (G!:30).

What a gracious provision is ours to access in our present journey! Truly, we can be conformed to Christ—from glory to glory—until that day at the consummation of all things, when we can wholly reclaim our true-self-in-Christ. Finally, when we come home to "glory," we are guaranteed never to fall short of it again—ever! Until then, as we daily find ourselves immersed in the concurrent experience of our true self and our false self within, we face the reality of tension, fully cognizant that our "deepest, truest self is not yet home" (IVL:50). In fact, the first step to our ongoing process of homecoming demands this continual claiming of our true self and the unmasking of our false self. In Thomas Merton's words, "To reach one's 'real self' one must, in fact, be delivered from that illusory and 'false self' whom we have created."[3]

Claiming Our True Self and Unmasking Our False Self

To begin the lifelong process of claiming our true self, we first must define what we mean by this "true self." More pointedly, how does Henri Nouwen perceive the true self? For starters, Nouwen insists that "we are not who we know ourselves to be, but who we are known to be by God."[4] Our true identity, therefore, is the one defined by God himself. So who are we according to God's precise view of us? The bottom line is that we are creatures made in the image of our Creator, "valued, valuing, and valuable"[5] beings whom God has loved and will continue to love from eternity to eternity.

Indeed "we are the beloveds of God," as Nouwen confidently declares repeatedly in almost all his speaking and writing. Unshakably, he understood Jesus' true identity as God's beloved Son (Matt 3:17) to be true of us as well and therefore something we can legitimately claim for ourselves (*BM*:68). As John Mogabgab, Nouwen's former teaching and research assistant at Yale, underscored, "This was for Henri the first truth about us, the truth beyond all biological, cultural, and psychological truths that accumulate around our identity."[6] So a practical question to ask is, how do we appropriate this positional reality into our experience?

SOLITUDE AS THE PLACE OF TENSION

Nouwen elevates the transformative role of solitude in the task of solidifying our core identity in God within our experience. "To claim the truth of ourselves," he points out, "we have to cling to our God in solitude as to the One who makes us who we are" (*BJ*:Aug 16). Solitude is truly a gift, for in it "we come to know our true nature, our true self, our true identity" (*CR*:28). For Nouwen, it is the true "way of the heart" wherein we can rightfully claim our belovedness.

Convinced that "our heart is at the center of our being human," Nouwen urges us to boldly enter into its mystery:

> Jesus desires to meet us in the seclusion of our own heart, to make his love known to us there, to free us from our fears, and to make our deepest self known to us. In the privacy of

our heart therefore, we can learn not only to know Jesus but, through Jesus, ourselves as well. (*LM*:68)

More to the point, as Nouwen clarifies, the more deeply we get to experience God's self-revealing love, the more our self-love deepens (*LM*:69). The late M. Basil Pennington was right:

The only way we really see ourselves is when we see ourselves reflected back to us from the eyes of one who truly loves us. But the only one who can reflect back to us the fullness of our beauty is God, for we are made in the very image of God. This is what we experience when we come to experience God in the contemplative experience.[7]

All of these experiential dynamics come to fruition within the contemplative context of solitude. Indeed, it is "the place we go in order to hear the truth about ourselves."[8] However, the moment we enter into this sacred place called solitude, we are apt to discover that it is suffused with mystery and the resultant tension. Left without much choice, we need to confront it if it is to be what it is meant to be—a venue for the continual conversion of our hearts.

Just what do we contend with when we delve into our interiority, into our so-called inner sanctuary? What can we realistically expect to face if we dare to enter into solitude with ourselves and God? Nouwen speaks plainly in revealing what awaits us there. He says, "In solitude we meet our demons, our addictions, our feelings of lust and anger, and our immense need for recognition and approval" (*BJ*:Jan 21). Yet he hastens to add, "But if we do not run away, we will meet there also the One who says, 'Do not be afraid. I am with you, and I will guide you through the valley of darkness'" (*BJ*:Ibid.). No wonder Nouwen identifies solitude elsewhere as "the place of the great *struggle* and the great *encounter*—the struggle against the compulsion of the false self, and the encounter with the loving God who offers himself as the substance of the new self" (*WOH*:26; italics mine).

Here Nouwen exposes the palpable tension accentuated by at least three sets of intertwining polarities—exact opposites that embody emerging expressions of both our true self and our false self: the coexistence of *light* and *darkness* in ourselves, underlining our *divinity* and our *humanity*, and further surfacing our inherent *dignity* and our natural *depravity* as God's created beings.

Engaging the Tension Within

From waking experience, we are acutely conscious of the oscillating, and at times, overlapping, tension between our true self and our false self. It is as though there is a civil war perennially raging inside us, evocative of what Paul refers to in his writings as the incessant battle between our flesh and the Spirit. Specifically, in Paul's terminology, the false self pertains to "life according to the flesh," while the true self aligns with "life according to the Spirit."[9] The latter refers to walking in the light of God's love and truth, and the former, to walking in darkness.

We are capable of walking in God's light because we are divinely endowed children of the God of light (Rom 8:15–16), yet we find ourselves also meandering in darkness due to our fallen nature. In this constant state of tension, we continue to witness to our sense of dignity on one hand, while miserably manifesting our depravity on the other. One need only be reminded of the dilemma Paul found himself caught up in, as graphically illustrated in Romans 7—the kind of driving tension we all, without a doubt, encounter in our respective journey experiences.

To be sure, the question of how to cope with this persistent and mounting tension besets many of us. How did Nouwen deal with it in practical ways?[10] Based upon his manner of handling it—much of it arising from his own struggles—I believe Nouwen is able to offer us a rich combination of helpful perspectives and concrete means by which we can, at the very least, learn to live with such tension ourselves.

In this regard, we will focus on two highly suggestive words we find in many of Nouwen's writings: *embrace* and *integrate*. While these correlated concepts may not register at once as sensible ways of dealing with the true self and the false self, we may realize sooner or later that they do in fact address a fundamental issue we cannot dismiss. Put simply, we can only really engage—tangibly and concretely—that which we first "embrace" and "integrate."

For example, the act of exclusion makes sense only against the backdrop of a prior embrace of something, in the same way that divorce can only occur within the context of a break from an established union. To further illustrate: one cannot possibly give away something he or she does not possess to begin with. One must own something first before one can dispose of it—or even do anything with it.

Applying this idea directly to the subject at hand, we cannot dismantle the false self unless we somehow view it as bound with the true self. If we are to seriously heed Merton's words about our need to "be delivered from that illusory and 'false self' whom we have created,"[11] we must, of necessity, recognize how that false self is inextricably attached to our true self. Thus, facing wholly who we are—that is, our personal constitution as humans—without splitting but consciously integrating our being is a crucial first step not only in terms of working our way through tension but even more so toward our movement to greater personal wholeness.

EMBRACING AND INTEGRATING OUR WHOLE SELF

Integral to the notion of loving ourselves is the capacity to accept and embrace the totality of who we are—good and bad, true and false. Lodged into our very depths is an ongoing inter-play of light and darkness. Unraveling the presence of the "dark corners as well as light spots" inside of us, according to Nouwen, heightens our inner familiarity with ourselves, thus enabling us to "feel at home in our own house" (SF:xx).

Learning to love who we are and to be truly friends with our-selves requires that we recognize the truth about ourselves, Nouwen contends. This necessitates an open acknowledgment on our part that simultaneously "we are beautiful but limited, rich but poor, generous but also worried about our security," among other things (BJ:Mar 21). Our inherent beauty, spiritual richness, and generosity of spirit all bring into focus the genuine sparks of the divine in us, while our natural limitations, our spiritual poverty, and our ingrained sense of insecurity betray our fallen humanity.

To embrace our true self is to acknowledge and claim "the sacredness of our being" with "souls [that] are embraced by a loving God" (BJ:Mar 21). Truly all of us are endowed with "divinity"—something that the Psalmist acknowledged with great awe when he queried God: "What are human beings that you are mindful of them, mortals that you care for them? Yet you have made them a little lower than God, and crowned them with glory and honor" (Ps 8:4–5). In a similar vein, Nouwen issues a confident reminder about our real status before God, which we would do well to take to heart:

> Your true identity is as a child of God. This is the identity you have to accept. Once you have claimed it and settled in it, you can live in a world that gives you much joy as well as pain. You can receive the praise as well as the blame that comes to you as an opportunity for strengthening your basic identity, because the identity that makes you free is anchored beyond all human praise and blame. (*IVL*:70)

Contrary to how most of us have allowed the world to shape our identity—via the distorted belief that "we are what we do, we are what others say about us, we are what we have" (*HN*:134)—God declares unequivocally who we are: not merely children of God, but *beloved* children of God. Our belovedness expresses in a genuine way the truth of our existence: loved creatures possessing both glory and limitations (*SD*:31).

To recognize limitations is to squarely face our humanity, which is, on all counts, imperfect. Our fallen humanity is the vehicle through which the subtle workings of the false self get contained and expressed. Pennington and Nouwen both agree that, at base, "the construct of the false self...is made up of what I have, what I do, and what others think of me"[12]—a falsity many of us have unwittingly bought into even though it runs counter to our God-given identity.

The moment we consent to such falsehood to dominate our own view of ourselves, we imperceptibly cloud our understanding and experience of God's unchanging love for us. Worse, we may end up disregarding it altogether. Nouwen himself confessed:

> The real sin is to deny God's first love for me, to ignore my original goodness. Because without claiming that first love and that original goodness for myself, I lose touch with my true self and embark on the destructive search among the

wrong people and in the wrong places for what can only be found in the house of my Father. (*RPS*:107)

This reveals the need for us to embrace not only our true self but our false self as well. If we don't, we will most likely fail to detect the false self's intricate dynamics—the exclusive ways our "flesh" operates within us (totally independent of God and dependent upon our natural inclinations). In essence, our flesh expresses itself in manifold ways, consistent with our unique personality, such that it is probably more precise to refer to our false self in its plurality—our many false selves.

A crucial aspect of embracing our numerous false selves is the ability to name them one by one as accurately as possible. Just as author Sue Monk Kidd explains, "By naming the inner patterns that imprison us, we come to know them more fully and obtain a certain power over them."[13] Appealing to some memorable lines in Arthur Miller's *After the Fall*, Kidd goes on to say that the process of naming our false selves requires us to "bend down to the broken, horrible faces in ourselves and kiss each one." What she emphasizes is the fact that "only by confronting the false selves and embracing them can we liberate the True Self."[14] We are released and empowered to live out of our true self as we are delivered from the clutches of the false self in us. Such deliverance happens when we first confront, then embrace the imposing reality of our false self.

Embracing our false self also results in us becoming more sharply aware of how cut off our humanity is from our divinity. In one of the spiritual memos he wrote to himself during a particularly dark period in his journey, Nouwen expressed this stark reality:

A split between divinity and humanity has taken place in you. With your divinely endowed center you know God's will, God's way, God's love. But your humanity is cut off from that. Your many human needs for affection, attention, and consolation are living apart from your divine sacred place. Your call is to let those two parts of yourself come together again. (*IVL*:7)

In short, we need integration—or perhaps reintegration—of that which we are always so inclined to split off. "In order to become full human beings," Nouwen further clarifies, "we have to claim the totality of our experience; we come to maturity by integrating not only the light but also the dark side of our story into our self-hood" (*LC*:29–30). Essentially, Nouwen is saying that all our experiences—good and bad—are ultimately useful and therefore need to be factored into our pursuit of wholeness and integration.

In case some of us are wondering what this kind of integration means and how it might look for us when applied, Carolyn Whitney-Brown, who was part of the L'Arche Daybreak community for the last six years before Nouwen passed away, helps us to see Nouwen's take on it:

> This was the theme of Henri's life: the stuff we might want to burn or toss out of our lives and hearts is the fertile material that makes us who we are, that will enlarge our hearts, that will draw us into community with compassion and maturity. But it takes work and grace to make our compulsions and aggression and resentment and fear into useful material integrated into our lives.[15]

As an example of how this actually works, Nouwen calls forth the novel idea of befriending our inner enemies, such as the unruly energies residing in our lust and anger. Our usual knee-jerk reaction each time we feel such energies overpowering us is to aggressively fight them tooth and nail. Deep within we are hoping against hope that the driving forces of lust and anger will just slowly evaporate by warding them off with all our might. Here Nouwen offers an unusual suggestion to arrest our so-called inner enemies:

> Instead of pushing our lust and anger away as unwelcome guests, we can recognize that our anxious, driven hearts need some healing. Our restlessness calls us to look for the true inner rest where lust and anger can be converted into a deeper way of loving. (*BJ*:Feb 3)

Nouwen believed that it is possible for our negative energies to actually be re-channeled to become more positive forces. He saw this not so much as eradicating our strong passions and desires as ordering them to serve a different purpose—constructive instead of destructive. We can only do this if and when we are deeply in touch with and able to listen well to what is going on inside of us—in the very topography of our being.

Again, this is where we can gravitate to solitude as a useful, revelatory vehicle through which we can process our internal energy while engaging our God-given senses and imagination, as opposed to merely exercising our will power to gain control of ourselves. Recognizing the sheer futility of will power to effect internal change in us, author Eugene Peterson insists that the wise use of our imagination is what will pull us into its field of reality, thereby producing real and deep conviction in our hearts.[16]

Such an imaginative process involves not just adjusting or reframing our minds, but creatively integrating our diverse energies, which, once sorted out internally, can lead to our envisioned change—one that emerges from the inside out. No amount of will power, no matter how strong our exertion of it is, can effect this level of change in us. The very act of "befriending" our inner demons requires quite a bit of internal exercise of the imagination, which connects with our deepest desires and longings, if indeed the goal is to facilitate a true change of heart.

Nouwen's concept of change is far deeper and much more nuanced than the idea of psyching ourselves up to rid ourselves of our shadow side. Neither is it a firm resolve to cut ourselves off from all that we find dark and negative in our life. On the contrary, Nouwen welcomed and embraced the conviction that "the whole spiritual life is a constant choice to let [our] negative spiritual experiences become an opportunity for conversion and renewal."[17] In fact, anything and everything that encompasses us and our experiences can prove to be vital resources, as well as instruments for our ongoing transformation. In God's economy, nothing is ever wasted, but all is redeemable.

Sue Monk Kidd echoes this idea in her metaphorical concept of "spiritual whittling," where, as we attempt to whittle away aspects of ourselves that do not quite resemble our true selves, we need not throw away the shavings. "Transformation happens," Kidd stresses, "not by rejecting...parts of ourselves but by gathering them up and integrating them. Through this process we reach a new wholeness."[18]

On the surface, this seems like a peculiar way of dealing with the inherent tension brought on by the spiritual polarity of our true self and our false self! On a much deeper, decidedly nondualistic level, however, it makes great sense. Once we learn to own ourselves—all of who we are—and open ourselves to God's deep transforming work within us, we become freer to give of ourselves in the service of others.

This ushers us to the next set of spiritual polarities we need to grapple with—"self-owning and self-giving"—which is critically related to this first one in that they both focus on the essential task of claiming our true self. In fact, the first set provides the foundation necessary for our exploration of the next one, further reinforcing the tension-filled journey in which we are all caught up.

⚘

True Self/False Self

FOR PERSONAL REFLECTION

1. As I enter into solitude, can I discern the presence of tension within me? How would I describe the reality of what I am experiencing about God and myself?

2. What specifically would it mean for me to embrace and claim my authentic self? What difference would that make in my personal journey?

3. Can I name accurately and honestly the many false selves I have constructed in my life? Am I able to detect how they manifest themselves in the way I relate to others? In the way I relate to God?

Suggested Reflective Exercise

PRAYER MANTRA

You may wish to pray this mantra slowly throughout your day for whatever duration you desire as a way to internalize the truth of your identity in God:

I am God's beloved,
a
valued,
valuing,
and
valuable
being
whom God loves
now
and forever!

CHAPTER TWO

Self-Owning and Self-Giving

> You cannot give yourself to others if you do not own your-
> self, and you can only truly own yourself when you have
> been fully received in unconditional love.
>
> Henri Nouwen, *The Inner Voice of Love*

Many of us have heard the familiar saying that some people are
out of control of their own self because their self is the one con-
trolling them. Who among us has not had episodes in our lives
where we have completely lost control of our personal bearing?
To be sure, we certainly can relate from each of our own experiences of this nature.

Such an "out-of-control" type of experience is bound to happen
when we lack what most psychologists refer to as a healthy ego
strength—the kind that enables us to have the inner capacity to exercise self-control versus being controlled externally, either by others
or by the circumstances around us. No doubt, there is a kernel of
truth to this, but it is important to qualify what constitutes this so-
called ego strength from a thoroughly Christian perspective.

As obvious as it may sound, one can only masterfully control
that which one intrinsically possesses or owns. In other words, we
need to possess a strong sense of self. To be more explicit, we have
to have a true sense of our authentic self in order to live authentically as human beings. Sadly, far too many people lead inau-
thentic lives because they choose to function out of their false

selves, many times without even being conscious of it. The false self is embedded so deeply that it becomes the default mode.

The Necessity of Self-Knowledge

People can go through life without ever deepening their level of self-awareness. The sobering truth is, that is how some have chosen to live life, content with superficial awareness of who they are. Evidently, these are the ones who cling to the adage that "life goes better the less you know." To an extent, that works for many, at least for a time. The refusal to know and confront the reality of one's self could well function as an effective way of managing the self. The only problem is, all too often, it backfires. People can't "control" and manage something that they really are not genuinely in control of. And they cannot possibly control what they do not fully own. Self-ownership, though, only takes place within the evolving context of self-knowledge. It follows therefore that one must know oneself truthfully before one can even technically "own" oneself; self-knowledge is a prerequisite to self-possession.

KNOWING ONESELF IN GOD

Let me emphasize that I am not referring to self-knowledge here for its own sake. When we point to self-knowledge, it must always be in direct relation to God—meaning that we only come to know ourselves in truth through our encounter with God (CR:29). As well, we encounter God as we encounter our deepest self, where God can be encountered most deeply. Thus, knowing self and knowing God inevitably intertwine and are interdependent.[1]

By directly stating "you cannot know God if you don't even know who you are,"[2] Henri Nouwen is foremost invoking who we really are by virtue of the *imago Dei*. We are the image of God and we can only know God via that image implanted in us by God himself. As we connect to God's image in us, we are enabled to connect to the very reality of the God behind this image. Nouwen sums it up for himself: "I am hidden in God and I have to find myself in that relationship."[3]

Once again, Nouwen directs our attention back to the vital importance of solitude as it relates to the pursuit of finding and knowing our God-imaged self:

> Solitude, silence, and prayer are often the best ways to self-knowledge. Not because they offer solutions for the complexity of our lives but because they bring us in touch with our sacred center, where God dwells. (*BJ*:Mar 22)

Needless to say, people who are not in touch with their sacred center cannot be in touch with the God who dwells within it. The desert fathers—whose deep spirituality Nouwen specifically wrote about—exhibited familiarity with this interior practice of self-knowing. The moment they entered into solitude in their physical cell, they likewise engaged their symbolic "cell"—what Henri Nouwen called the inner sanctuary of their being (cf. *RPS*:16–18). In the process, these proficient contemplatives discovered "the new alphabet of the heart" while acquiring increased skill in "exegeting" the movements of their own heart through discernment.[4]

As we ourselves engage in this same introspective work of descending into our own hearts to enter our inner world—to use Augustine's familiar rhetoric in his *Confessions*—we are aided by no less than the searchlight of God's Spirit. We can echo the very prayer of the Psalmist: "Search me, O God, and know my heart; test me and know my thoughts. See if there is any wicked way in me, and lead me in the way everlasting" (Ps 139:23–24). We are able to plumb the depths of our hearts with God himself guiding the process. God is the one who helps us to know ourselves—the hurtful way of the false self included. Recognizing our false self reinforces our need to be led "in the way everlasting" of the true self which, by every means possible, we must affirm on a continual basis.

AFFIRMING ONESELF IN GOD

To affirm our self in direct relationship to God is to realize that our real identity is inherently spiritual, because it is rooted in the *imago Dei*. In a way, affirming our spiritual identity precedes the act of claiming our true self. So what precisely must we first affirm about our self?

Henri Nouwen notes that much of what governs our behavior is the nagging question, "Who are we?" While we rarely ask this question formally, we nevertheless live it out concretely on a daily basis. For the most part, the kind of identity many of us have come to affirm, according to Nouwen, is largely based on success, popularity, and power—symbolic translations of what we do, what others say about us, and what we have. All of this is illusory and is nothing but a false identity, according to Nouwen.

The only thing worth affirming is what God ascribes to you and me: "You are not what the world makes you; but you are children of God" (*HN*:134–135). Even more explicitly, we are the *beloved* children of God, as Nouwen never tires of repeating. He cautions us never to allow ourselves to be pulled out of our true self. This is his resounding advice: "Protect your innocence by holding on to the truth: you are a child of God and deeply loved" (*IVL*:77).

Henri Nouwen likes to refer to the reality of God loving us as God's first love. He enjoins us to keep opening ourselves to this first love as a crucial part of our own self-affirmation:

> God has given you a beautiful self. There God dwells and loves you with the first love, which precedes all human love. You carry your own beautiful, deeply loved self in your heart. You can and must hold on to the truth of the love you were given. (*IVL*:29)

Admittedly, this is one challenge that remains difficult for many of us to incorporate into our experience. It is one thing to assent to it in our head; it is quite another to actually live out its truth, let alone allow ourselves to experience its deepest reality within our hearts.

Henri Nouwen himself would be the first to confess that he struggled with accepting this truth for most of his life. In fact, it took a very long time before it finally descended from his mind into his heart. But once he allowed it to settle deep down, this truth about God's first love became a genuine conviction of his heart, so much so that he felt compelled to affirm it with a contagious passion! Nouwen's later writings substantiate this life-altering experience for him. This newfound exercise in healthy self-acceptance and affirmation profoundly changed the course of his ministry.

Self-Affirmation and Self-Emptying

As much as self-affirmation is part of our total embrace of our spiritual identity in God, Henri Nouwen never looked at it as an end goal. The need to strengthen our view of ourselves to reflect God's true view of us transcends our preoccupation with our secure standing before God. Self-affirmation definitely points beyond who we are, or even whose we are, to what we are about—that is, to what we are designed for. As Nouwen categorically emphasizes, "[w]e are for others."[5]

Such emphasis forms the basis for Nouwen's balanced recognition of "the intangible tension between self-affirmation and self-denial, self-fulfillment and self-emptying, self-realization and self-sacrifice" (CM:52). This presupposes that there is in fact an "affirmed" self we can deny, empty out, and sacrifice for the sake of others. One cannot possibly deny a self that is not first affirmed to exist ontologically; one cannot empty a self that is not filled to begin with; and self-sacrifice is pointless if there is no real self to give up.

Despite their seeming polarity, Nouwen does not necessarily view self-affirmation and self-emptying as antithetical to each other. For indeed no one can give away what he or she does not have. No one can give oneself in love when one is not aware of oneself (CM:51). Nouwen illustrates this using Jesus as an example:

> Jesus lived thirty years in a simple family. There He became a man who knew who He was and where He wanted to go. Only then was He ready to empty Himself and give His life for others. (CM:52)

Nouwen applies this general principle to people in ministry by clarifying that ministers need to find their place in life, discover their own contribution, and affirm their own self. This they must do not to cling to it and claim it as their own unique property, but to offer their services to others, emptying themselves in order for God to work through them (CM:52).

Nouwen has described ministry in terms of a willingness to lay down one's life for others—not necessarily in a literal way but as a matter of identity. He has stressed that if a person is to lay down his or her life, that person must have a real "life" to lay down.[6] This correlates directly to the most concise definition of ministry Nouwen has ever articulated in his writings: ministry is all about "the giving of self" (G!:85). The big question is: "What 'self' do we give to others—our true self or our false self?" The reality is, we can only minister out of who we genuinely are. What enables us to minister with real depth and effectiveness is living out of our center, where our core identity is deeply lodged.[7]

The Polarity of Self-Owning and Self-Giving

All this brings us back to the creative tension we ought to maintain between the spiritual polarities of self-owning and self-giving, which is fundamentally premised upon Henri Nouwen's firm belief that you cannot give away anything you do not first own, like your "self" (*IVL*:65).[8] But you cannot own yourself unless you have staked a true claim on yourself. Nouwen says that what is needed is to "claim yourself for yourself, so that you can contain your needs within the boundaries of your self and hold them in the presence of those you love...True mutuality in love requires people who possess themselves and who can give to each other while holding on to their own identities" (*IVL*:9–10).

It follows that you are able only to claim that which you can authentically affirm about your self. In this regard, Nouwen issues a caution: "You cannot fully claim yourself when parts of you are still wayward. You have to acknowledge where you are and affirm that place" (*IVL*:53–54). Thus, the important tasks of claiming and affirming go hand in hand. Henri Nouwen declares that once you have claimed your own belovedness in God and have established appropriate boundaries to your love with your needs well contained, "you begin to grow into the freedom to give gratuitously" (*IVL*:11).

There is yet another component that interlocks with the combined imperatives of "owning," "claiming," and "affirming"—self-knowledge. Indeed, this is where we began our discussion of self-owning and self-giving, because it is foundational to a life of service for God. As we noted earlier, self-knowledge works in tandem with God-knowledge (both in terms of how God knows us and of how we come to know God). As David Benner qualifies, "true knowing of our self demands that we know our self as known by God."[9]

It is critical for us to know our self deeply enough that we know for certain what we are called to affirm, claim, and ultimately own. Such quality of knowing can pave the way to liberate us from our "inner dividedness" and motivate us to go deeper into our center—that is, "deeper into [our] heart and thus deeper into the heart of God" (*IVL*:51–52).

Only when we become confident that we are unconditionally received and loved by God can we freely love others. It is from this secure place that we are completely able to give of ourselves to the service of others (*IVL*:65). In a way, this embodies the unique freedom we enjoy as God's children. Nouwen reassures each of us: "The more you come to know yourself—spirit, mind, and body—as truly loved, the freer you will be to proclaim the good news" (*IVL*:75).

This liberating truth spills over into our relational dynamics, including most especially our friendships. Nouwen notes that friendship becomes a lot more freeing once we recognize the truth that we are deeply loved because then we are released to love others nonpossessively (*IVL*:80). Furthermore, knowing and owning this truth of our belovedness helps us escape the tyranny of self-rejection that plagues many of us, just as it tormented Nouwen himself for a large part of his life. Learning from his own painful experiences in the past, he entreats us to accept our own limitations yet claim our giftedness, enabling us to "live as an equal among equals" who can "give and receive true affection and friendship" without being possessive as well as obsessive (*IVL*:86–87).

The interrelated dynamics of knowing, affirming, claiming, and owning our ultimate identity in God extend even to the realm of our God-given calling as individuals. Through engaging in them, we are enabled to pursue "a vocation grounded in identity," one that empowers us to live the truth of our own uniqueness.[10] More importantly, these same dynamics propel us to follow our deepest calling in a way that benefits others. Foundationally, they provide us with a "solid inner base from which [we] can speak and act—without apologies—humbly but convincingly" (*IVL*:44) and give ourselves away to and for others.

For Henri Nouwen, this is what genuine ministry is about—a ministry that comes straight out of who we are, embodying the self we embrace as our very own, and therefore the same self we are able to give to others freely as a gift. Of this, Nouwen remained convinced: "One of the greatest gifts we can give others is ourselves" (*BJ*:Apr 14). And as we willingly do so, we stand to gain it back. Such is the great paradox of life. Giving our lives away for the sake of others—which Henri Nouwen himself considered to be "the greatest of all human acts"—is ultimately what will gain us back our lives (*BJ*:Apr 10).

Corollary to this is the similar polarity between *emptiness* and *fullness*, which Henri Nouwen construes as spiritual realities that interweave dynamically. Normally viewed as conceptual opposites, Nouwen insists that in the spiritual realm they transcend their seeming polarity: "In the spiritual life we find the fulfillment of our deepest desires by becoming empty for God" (*BJ*:May 13).

Here Nouwen turns our attention back to the supreme *kenotic* example of Jesus, who, although he possessed the fullness of God, emptied himself instead for our sake, finally to be exalted. As Nouwen put it, "He who had emptied and humbled himself was raised up and 'given the name above all other names'" (see Phil 2:7–9). Jesus' humble self-giving act emerged out of his own self—the full ownership and embrace of who he was as the beloved Son of God. Despite attempts by the devil to assault his true identity ("If you are the Son of God"), Jesus clung fiercely to who he knew himself to be (see Matt 4:1–11).

Jesus freely gave himself to and for others because he had a full self to give, one that he thoroughly possessed and securely owned. Henri Nouwen too became a man for others as he unreservedly gave to people all of himself—"a self anchored upon his true, spiritual identity before God as God's beloved."[11] Both showed us through their practical example how self-owning and self-giving can operate in fruitful tension.

There is, however, a significant aspect of the self that we own and give to others that we simply cannot dismiss. We need to factor into the equation the tensional reality that part of our self is wounded, bruised, and broken while simultaneously undergoing the process of healing, mending, and becoming whole. The next chapter focuses on this polar tension.

Self-Owning/Self-Giving

FOR PERSONAL REFLECTION

1. How can the combined practice of solitude, silence, and prayer aid me personally in my own pursuit of self-knowing?

2. What are some ways I can deeply engage in the process of self-acceptance and self-affirmation? What do I see as the positive consequences of doing so?

3. How do I understand and experience "my belovedness in God"? Why is it so crucial for me to embrace this reality in terms of how I give of myself to others?

Suggested Reflective Exercise

SELF INVENTORY

Do you love who you are? Can you truly affirm your true identity in God such that you can freely give your precious self away?

As you engage in this personal inventory, consider writing a short poem, a psalm, or a simple prayer to God expressing how you are deciding to fully embrace your self as the beloved of God.

Afterward, you may want to read aloud what you wrote about to yourself or choose to share it with someone you care for. Perhaps, you can even set it to music and create your own melody ("Sing a new song to the Lord").

Or simply offer to God whatever you composed as a sacrament of praise—a sacred reminder that you are deeply loved, and therefore, you can generously offer love to others!

CHAPTER THREE

Woundedness and Healing

When Jesus says, "It is not the healthy who need the doctor, but the sick" he affirms that only those who face their wounded condition can be available for healing and so enter into a new way of living.

Henri Nouwen, *The Living Reminder*

Despite our natural tendency to compartmentalize ourselves, our personhood remains a unity—that is, we are all at once a thinking, feeling, and acting being. There really is no way we can isolate each of our capacities as individuals from the others; all of them are interconnected. Our total human functioning is inevitably affected by our combined rationality, will, emotions, and actions as together they interact unceasingly within what we call our "self."

At the same time, psychologists call attention to the fact that our so-called self can easily fragment, scatter, and potentially disintegrate into many parts without us being fully conscious of it happening to us. The common expression "to collect oneself" speaks to the needful process of self-integration with which we must engage. However, this can be a difficult, if not impossible task if we are not cognizant of the many existing selves we have. As psychologist David Benner points out, "What we call 'I' is really a family of many part-selves" that we either conveniently ignore or dismiss altogether—especially the ones that make us feel vulnerable, such as our broken and wounded self.[1]

Benner could not be more emphatic in stating that

> Christian spirituality involves acknowledging all our part-selves, exposing them to God's love and letting him weave them into the new person he is making. To do this, we must be willing to welcome these ignored parts as full members of the family of self, giving them space at the family table and slowly allowing them to be softened and healed by love and integrated into the whole person we are becoming.[2]

Henri Nouwen takes Jesus' statement that it is not the healthy who need a doctor but the sick (Mark 2:17) to mean that it is nearly impossible for healing to be experienced by anyone who is unprepared to acknowledge his or her ailing condition. Only as we learn to face our wounded state can we ever hope to enter the path of healing and wholeness in our life. Woundedness and healing are never apart from each other; they invariably intersect as both interact constantly. Healing is effected to the extent that we are addressing our broken state. To the degree that we are able to live through our woundedness, we become disposed to experience the depth of healing we seek.

Facing and Living Our Woundedness

One might well ask, how can we possibly ignore our broken condition that we so obviously live out from day to day? But, in actuality, most of us do so, in both subtle and not-so-subtle ways. This process is called denial and it comes in myriad forms. In almost all cases, the deeper the wound, the stronger the denial we instinctively employ. Most of us tend to squirm out of our experience of pain. We all use our unique brands of spiritual sedatives and anesthetics that suit our temperaments to numb it out. Whatever painkillers we resort to, the aim is the same: to minimize, if not altogether eradicate, the discomfort of dealing with our broken self. Most succeed to an extent, but never for long.

Many have learned to gloss over their wounded self deliberately by employing their more confident, competent part-selves in an effort to overcompensate for the self they would rather hide.

Such overcompensation can easily translate into a persona that we don quite creatively. There is truth to the familiar Jungian maxim that says the darker our shadow, the brighter the persona that we learn to ingeniously put on.

Denying our fractured condition is really an exercise in futility since it will remain as our inescapable lot. The reality will keep staring us in the eye, one way or the other. We might as well abandon the illusion that we have what it takes to avoid dealing with it. Of course, that is easier said than done. But once we are afforded the chance, even the slightest, to acknowledge our woundedness, it will be to our sure advantage to readily admit that we cannot totally cure ourselves. We can only receive and experience God's healing presence when we humbly confess our utter powerlessness to alter our condition solely on our own (*IVL*:30).

Henri Nouwen points to two extremes we would do well to avoid in confronting the state of our own woundedness: "being completely absorbed in [our] pain and being distracted by so many things that [we] stay far away from the wound [we] want to heal" (*IVL*:3). We all know how pain can be so self-absorbing that before we realize it, we find ourselves wallowing in it. When we do so, we are stuck with our sorry state, eventually giving up hope that there is in fact a way out of it. On the other hand, we can mobilize our energies to avoid attending to it. Both ways will only prove unhealthy in the end.

ENTERING INTO OUR PAIN

"The first response, then, to our brokenness is to face it squarely and befriend it," Henri Nouwen emphasizes. Healing can start the moment we step toward our pain rather than away from it. Nouwen urges us to "dare overcome our fear and become familiar with it" as an intrinsic part of our being (*LB*:75–76). This requires that we name our pain and see it for what it is without explaining it away. Pain can constitute any number of phenomena for us: sufferings we have wittingly or unwittingly imposed upon ourselves or even upon others; wounds inflicted upon us by others; the unfulfilled desires and longings that haunt us; the agonies and sorrows we feel over our personal losses; or simply the universal pain that is the consequence of living in a fallen world along with its resultant array of imperfections. For Nouwen, pain goes with the territory of suffering from our wounded, broken situation.

Only when we are willing to go into the very place of our pain and learn gradually to live through it can we divest it of its power over us. Nouwen well understands the qualms you and I have about the dreaded idea of entering into our own places of hurt:

> To go back to that place is hard, because you are confronted there with your wounds as well as with your powerlessness to heal yourself. You are so afraid of that place that you think of it as a place of death. Your instinct for survival makes you run away and go looking for something else that can give you a sense of at-homeness. (*IVL:*26)

Nouwen counsels us to believe that our situated pain is never the final experience—"that beyond it is a place where [we] are being held in love." If we do not hang on to that belief, it becomes too dangerous to attempt to reenter our place of pain, only to feel its rawness. That can only distract us from where we should be headed ultimately—which is the new place of healing (*IVL:*Ibid.).

Most of us, understandably, do not relish the idea of staying with our hurts, our state of brokenness, our gnawing feelings of loneliness, our nagging sense of incompleteness. Nouwen, however, cautions us not to fall into the tendency either to "nurse our pain or to escape into fantasies about people who will take it away." Instead, he encourages us to face and contain our pain in a safe place where it can be available for God to touch and heal it (*IVL:*47).

OWNING OUR PAIN

Once we gain the requisite courage to enter into our pain, face it, and stay with it for a while, then we are able to reach the point where we can fully own it. To own our pain is to bring it home deep into our hearts, to allow it to settle down there. Henri Nouwen alerts us: "As long as your wounded part remains foreign to your adult self, your pain will injure you as well as others." On the other hand, if we incorporate our pain into our self, chances are it will yield fruit not only in our heart but in others as well. Nouwen believes that this is what Jesus is referring to when he asks you and me to be willing to carry our own crosses:

He encourages you to recognize and embrace your unique suffering and to trust that your way to salvation lies therein. Taking up your cross means, first of all, befriending your wounds and letting them reveal to you your own truth. (*IVL*:88)

Indeed, we have our own version of pain and suffering that is uniquely ours to claim. As Nouwen puts it, "Our brokenness is always lived and experienced as highly personal, intimate and unique" (*LB*:71). Only we can bear and carry our own crosses. Yet as we do so—in fact, as we learn to do so steadfastly—the potential benefit for others can be far-reaching, perhaps more than we may imagine.

Owning our pain—"that is, integrat[ing] [our] pain into [our] way of being in the world," according to Henri Nouwen—also prepares our hearts so we can talk about it more openly and freely in a way that serves others (*IVL*:72). How? Through our own struggle with accepting it we end up lending other people our hope even as they witness the strength by which we cope with the unwelcome interruptions that pain brings. People do identify and connect with a reality we ourselves have learned to embrace.

The bold and honest embrace of our pain also entails the imperative for us to live our wounds through. Nouwen poses to us an option worth sorting out—the challenge of "*living* [our] wounds through instead of *thinking* them through." In letting our wounds descend into our hearts we will discover the truth that we will not in fact be destroyed by them, since "[our] heart is greater than [our] wounds" (*IVL*:110). Without fully realizing it, we are actually able to minister more deeply to other wounded souls through the undiluted transparency of our experience, to which many surely can relate.

Additionally, the pain we learn to own and live through allows us to participate concretely with the pain of all of humanity. While it is true that our pain is unique in many different ways, it is equally true that it does bear a general resemblance to the universal pain everyone else experiences one way or the other. Henri Nouwen sheds additional light on this seemingly paradoxical case:

We can truly listen to the pains of the world because there we can recognize them not as strange and unfamiliar pains, but as pains that are our own. There we can see that what is most universal is most personal and that, indeed, nothing human is strange to us. (*RO*:58)

In a revealing way, "our wounds allow us to enter into a deep solidarity with our wounded brothers and sisters" (*BJ*:Jul 9). "It is this inner solidarity which...makes compassion possible," Nouwen hastens to add (*RO*:59).

Out of this acquired posture of compassion arising from such deepening recognition of our own pain, we are consequently emboldened to step out of our isolation, engage in true compassion (*IVL*:104), and begin fellowshipping with the suffering others. In view of our shared reality, we are naturally drawn in to what Nouwen calls "a fellowship of the weak" (*HN*:40–41), enveloped by a community—a community of the wounded that is simultaneously a healing community. Henri Nouwen explicates its dynamic outworking:

A Christian community is therefore a healing community not because wounds are cured and pains are alleviated, but because wounds and pains become openings or occasions for a new vision. Mutual confession then becomes a mutual deepening of hope, and sharing weaknesses becomes a reminder to one and all of the coming strength. (*WH*:94)

Here we see clearly how woundedness and healing cannot, in the strictest sense, be separate—particularly within their communal context. Moreover, when situated and seen as the blessing that indeed they are, we encounter their intertwining realities not just in connection with the healing of wounds but of the wounds that heal as well.

Healing of Wounds

None of us should feel stuck or should wallow in our woundedness, as it is never meant to be our permanent state. All of us can, and must, latch on to "the reality of an actual healing which is taking place provisionally and will most certainly take place finally."[3] Healing does incorporate a present and a future dimension, which unquestionably overlap, as we are given both a taste of it in this present life and a guarantee of its completeness when we enter into eternity. Healing is just as powerfully real as the wounds that can tend to overpower us.

Healing is very much a potent force in our day-to-day existence—regardless of whether we are aware of it or not. We do have an innate capacity to heal ourselves. And it is quite possible for a certain measure of healing to take place in our lives—emotionally, mentally, and even physically—without us fully recognizing it. It takes a great deal of attentiveness to sort through what is going on in our lives within the realm of felt experience, and none of us are able to maintain such attentiveness at all times.

However, for true healing to be more meaningfully felt and experienced at its deepest level, we need to be fully awake to the whole process involved. Healing must touch the domain of our consciousness. Essentially, this means that the vast field of our memories—that, in all likelihood, contain wounding of all sorts—must be plowed and penetrated through. Persuaded of the utmost importance of attending to our memories, Nouwen postulates:

> We are healed first of all by letting [our memories] be available, by leading them out of the corner of forgetfulness and by remembering them as part of our life stories. What is forgotten is unavailable, and what is unavailable cannot be healed. (*LR*:22)

If we fail to activate our forgotten memories, they emerge as "independent forces that can exert a crippling effect on our functioning as human beings" (*LR*:21). We can end up becoming disconnected from ourselves, and worse, aborting our potential to be whole.

There is yet another crucial aspect to our process of healing that Henri Nouwen lays out for us: the necessity of making connections. The connections are twofold: with the suffering of our fellow human beings and with God's own suffering. The first connection has already been briefly alluded to earlier on in conjunction with the tasks of owning and living through our pain. All the same, Nouwen assures us that "real healing comes from realizing that [our] own particular pain is a share in humanity's pain"

(*IVL*:104). Likewise, we need to recognize it as "rising from the depth of the human condition which all [people] share" (*WH*:88). Not only is this kind of "horizontal" connection vital, but we need to make an equally important "vertical" connection with God's suffering in and through the person Christ.

To this end, Nouwen submits that healing entails a recognition that our wounds are connected to God's own suffering—that is, our human story intersects with the divine story. A great part of our healing process then revolves around the ongoing realization that "our pains are part of a greater pain, that our sorrows are part of a greater sorrow, that our experience is part of the great experience of him who said, 'But was it not ordained that the Christ should suffer and so enter into the glory of God?' [cf. Luke 24:26]" (*LR*:25). Bear in mind that we all participate in a grand story much larger and bigger than our little stories. And here is the wonderful news: Just as we are privileged to share in the suffering of Christ, we shall also partake of his glory. Until then, we await our complete healing and wholeness even as we are given a foretaste of it in the here and now.

Wounds That Heal

The healing of our wounds, like the fact of our own woundedness, is very much an ongoing reality with which we all engage. In his compiled work *Turning My Mourning into Dancing*, Henri Nouwen delivers a helpful perspective worth taking to heart: "One of life's great questions centers not on what happens to us, but rather, how we will live in and through whatever happens."[4] Our broken and wounded state is always bound to present us with inherent limitations and ever-increasing challenges. But as author Wayne Muller penetratingly asks: "how will we hold them, how will we be changed, how will they shape us, what will we bring to the healing of them, what, if anything, will be born in its place?"[5]

There is no question for Nouwen that the foremost route to the healing of our wounds—that is, the way out of our hurts, pains, and suffering—is "*in* and *through*" them. A more direct way of stating it is this: the healing of wounds is via the wounds that heal.

While we at first may consider our wounds nothing more than liabilities, they can in fact turn into spiritual assets. They transform into wounds that heal—healing us and healing others. Here we can see how our own experience of brokenness can serve as a powerful witness to other brokenhearted people who long as we all do not just to be healed, but to be agents of healing for others. What paves this agency of healing? When our woundedness is converted into such kind of blessing, healing becomes even more potent.

That woundedness is itself a source of healing is by no means just a theoretical claim. Without a doubt, Henri Nouwen's life exemplified this truth quite tangibly. His own protracted experience of anguish is said not only to have "fueled his genius"[6] but generated untold blessings for himself and countless others whose lives he was able to touch directly or indirectly. In this light, poet Wallace Stevens's enigmatic remark makes sense: "The imperfect is our paradise."[7]

BLESSEDNESS OF BROKENNESS

Henri Nouwen focuses our attention on the fact that we can claim our woundedness as our "unique way to glory" (*IVL*:97) and make our brokenness into "the gateway to joy" (*LB*:78). Quoting the great Augustine who remarked, "In my deepest wound I see your glory and it dazzles me," Richard Rohr can only conclude that "Our wound is our way through."[8] Indeed, the path toward our eventual wholeness is precisely through our own woundedness—as counterintuitive as it sounds.[9] As Nouwen testifies, "My own experience with anguish has been that facing it and living it through, is the way to healing" (*LB*:77). How does this happen and get translated into concrete reality in our experience?

There are inherent sacramental blessings contained within our broken condition if we can see past its ugly face. To borrow Nouwen's familiar language, once we choose to move beyond its "opaqueness" and into "transparency" by contemplating its deeper reality, we will soon realize that our brokenness does not have the final say in our lives; wholeness does. Our woundedness is reckoned but a means and never as the end. Nouwen shares this helpful viewpoint:

> The deep truth is that our human suffering need not be an obstacle to the joy and peace we so desire, but can become, instead, the means *to* it. The great secret of the spiritual

life…is that everything we live, be it gladness or sadness, joy or pain, health or illness, can all be part of the journey toward the full realization of our humanity. (*LB*:77)

Despite the severity of our broken state, all of our shattered pieces can prove vital to our own personal integration.

Nouwen stands convinced that we are only able to befriend our woundedness as we learn how to see it as a blessing instead of a curse. "Living our brokenness under the curse," he avers, "means that we experience our pain as a confirmation of our negative feelings about ourselves" (*LB*:78). Each time something bad happens to us, or when we get a raw deal out of life, we end up evaluating our circumstances in accordance with this distorted thinking that we must be cursed. Consequently, we start nurturing unwarranted fears in our hearts that further prevent us from facing our woundedness head-on. This, in turn, only delays the prospect for our true healing.

Thus, instead of operating under the predication of a curse, Henri Nouwen summons us to reframe our thinking by consciously seeing our brokenness as a blessing.

> The great spiritual call of the Beloved Children of God is to pull their brokenness away from the shadow of the curse and put it under the light of the blessing. [G]reat and heavy burdens become light and easy when they are lived in the light of the blessing. What seemed intolerable becomes a challenge. What seemed a reason for depression becomes a source of purification. What seemed punishment becomes gentle pruning. What seemed rejection becomes a way to a deeper communion. (*LB*:79)

While none of our brokenness will ever disappear completely or even be minimized during our lifetime, Nouwen is nevertheless certain that "embracing it and bringing it into the light of the One who calls us the Beloved can make our brokenness shine like a diamond" (*LB*:81).

What can prove to be the ultimate blessing is to be able to put our woundedness in the service of others. This we can do by following in Nouwen's footsteps and becoming exactly what he was: a wounded healer.

BEING A WOUNDED HEALER

Writing from the perspective of the Christian East with such deep appreciation for Henri Nouwen's popularized image of the wounded healer, Gregory Jensen highlights this fundamental insight from Scripture:

> A Christian is able to be a wounded healer not simply for human reasons of psychology or sociology, but for reasons of Christology. Christ is himself the icon of the wounded healer, of that man of sorrows who bore our wounds and whose stripes we are healed (see Is 53).[10]

Jensen also rightly notes that Nouwen did not split the famous Jungian archetype of the wounded healer in that the individual was never viewed merely as "wounded or a healer, not broken or whole...but both together."[11] In Nouwen's own words, each one of us "is called to be the wounded healer, the one who must look after [our] own wounds but at the same time be prepared to heal the wounds of others." In short, we are considered "both the wounded minister and the healing minister" (*WH*:82).

How can we be an effective wounded healer ourselves? Henri Nouwen notes two specific ways: first is to "find the freedom to step over our wounds" and allow ourselves to fall "into the safe embrace of a God whose love will heal all [our] wounds" (*HN*:45); second is to tend to our wounds first by letting the healing presence of others minister to us. In allowing that to happen, "we can discover our own gifts of healing" (*BJ*:Jul 9), Nouwen says, and be enabled, through "our own bandaged wounds," to listen wholeheartedly to others in their suffering. He further clarifies what this type of healing service entails:

> A wounded healer is someone who can listen to a person in pain without having to speak about his or her own wounds... Mostly it is better not to direct a suffering person's attention to ourselves. (*BJ*:Jul 10)

In essence, a true wounded healer is one who has learned to balance creatively the inner tension of his or her own woundedness on one hand and the capacity to heal on the other. Wounded healers know what it means to embrace both realities in their experience and as such, they can move out of themselves with ease and reach out to others with an even greater sense of confidence.

❦

Woundedness/Healing

FOR PERSONAL REFLECTION

1. How can I bravely enter into my pain and own it in such a way that it can bring me closer to wholeness and healing?

2. What will it entail for me personally to live my wounds through instead of thinking them through?

3. Instead of reckoning it as a source of shame, how may I put my own woundedness in the service of others?

Suggested Reflective Exercise

PROCESS THE PROCESS

In dealing with your own pain and woundedness, imagine walking yourself through the following process of healing. At your own pace, slowly and prayerfully,

Enter into it...
   Face it...
      Stay with it...
         Own it...
            Connect it...

Listen to your heart and notice feelings of ease, points of resistance, or areas of surrender. Journal the process to help you sort out either the propellants and/or the impediments to your own path to healing.

PART II

Living with *Outward* Polarities
(Ministerial Tensions)

The careful balance between silence and words, withdrawal and involvement, distance and closeness, solitude and community forms the basis of the spiritual life and should therefore be the subject of our most personal attention.

Henri Nouwen, *Out of Solitude*

CHAPTER FOUR

Solitude and Community

Through the discipline of solitude we discover space for God in our innermost being. Through the discipline of community we discover a place for God in our life together. Both disciplines belong together precisely because the space within us and the space among us are the same place.

Henri Nouwen, *Making All Things New*

The subjects of solitude and community—taken both separately and together—are staple features in almost all of Henri Nouwen's writings. Not surprisingly, Nouwen discussed them not as abstract constructs but as living realities that galvanized his own journey experience. Yet they posed the greatest challenge for him to balance.

Nouwen was very much "a person of paradox who indeed had a profoundly contemplative heart but who needed to be constantly on the move, a man filled with immense energies that were difficult to harness."[1] Almost always he found himself amidst the tension of his competing desires to either withdraw from or engage with people—desires that were of equal significance as propellants for the way he expressed his spirituality.

Nouwen genuinely enjoyed being alone with and for God in solitude. Following Jesus' own example from the Gospels, he consistently carved out time in his daily schedule to quietly be present before God's presence. He also retreated from his busy life on a periodic basis in order to spend more extended and focused times of contemplation. Unquestionably, Nouwen highly valued the spiritual discipline of solitude, without which he believed no real transformation was possible. Throughout his life, he lived by this conviction.

At the same time, Nouwen vigorously latched onto the experience of community as if it were his lifeline. His desire for connection with others ran deep, and belongingness motivated his entire existence. Community became for him a safe refuge as well as a place of growth and healing, despite its own share of challenges. For Nouwen, the notion of journeying outside the context of community was simply an inconceivable one. Community was not a luxury; it was an absolute necessity—and Nouwen translated this reality into his experience. He had his spiritual life fleshed out with, through, and for others, always mindful that spirituality itself is irreducibly a communal affair—not locked into a privatized and interiorized practice. Solitude and community generated for Nouwen a rhythmic tension between the inward and the outward spiritual dynamics that required a critical balancing act.

Dynamic Interaction between Solitude and Community

Dietrich Bonhoeffer, whose classic writing on Christian community had obviously influenced Nouwen, addressed the interrelationship between aloneness in solitude and connectedness in community:

> *Let him* [sic] *who cannot be alone beware of community.* He will only do harm to himself and to the community. But the reverse is also true: *Let him who is not in community beware of being alone.* Only in the fellowship do we learn to be rightly alone and only in aloneness do we learn to live rightly in the fellowship. It is not as though the one preceded the other; both begin at the same time, namely with the call of Jesus Christ.[2]

Indeed, we are summoned to actively engage in both the spiritual practice of self-withdrawal and communal engagement. We cannot have one without the other. Henri Nouwen understood both as tightly bound with each other.

Solitude, which Nouwen pictured as "the garden for our hearts," is supposed to be "the place where our aloneness can bear fruit" (*BJ*:Jan 21). How so? Nouwen believed it is via solitude that our hearts experience what it means to be solidly grounded and centered in God. As we allow the discipline of solitude to propel us continually to claim our own center, it simultaneously emboldens us to summon others to also claim their own—thus inevitably strengthening the experience of our communal reality together (*BJ*:Jan 22). Instead of making demands or clinging dependently on one another—consequently draining the life out of community—solitude enables us to accord due respect for others' uniqueness and thus build community (*BJ*:Jan 18).

Nouwen warns that if we fail to claim our belovedness in God through solitude, we are bound to expect others within the community to make us feel loved. Far from the mistaken notion that community is about lonely people grabbing onto other lonely people, in reality, "community is solitude greeting solitude" (*SD*:114). It is a sacred, mutual encounter of "beloveds of God" welcoming one another and deepening their intimacy with each other (see *CR*:13).

There are some very practical implications to Nouwen's prime conviction that solitude serves as a fertile ground from which community grows. He explains its communal outworking:

> With solitude...we learn to depend on God, who calls us together in love, in whom we can rest, and through whom we can enjoy and trust each other even when our ability to express ourselves to each other is limited. With solitude, we are protected against the harmful effects of mutual suspicions, and our words and actions become more joyful expressions of an already existing trust, rather than a subtle way of asking for proof of trustworthiness. With solitude we can experience each other as different manifestations of a love that transcends all of us. (*CR*:13;14;15)

Henri Nouwen places the utmost significance on "formation to life in community" (*SD*:15). He expresses his own desperate longing for such formational quality unequivocally: "I needed to be in community where my spiritual life would deepen in relationship to others" (SD:116). To Nouwen, spirituality apart from life together in community is simply unworkable, if not thoroughly impossible. It is precisely in the context of community that we grow in our capacity to forgive each other, celebrate our full humanity, and consequently learn "how all love is connected, expressed, and lived out" (SD:123;125).

Holistically speaking, our life with God is sustained not just by the periodic practice of abandonment via self-withdrawal; neither is it nurtured merely by availability via consistent communal engagement. Again, for Henri Nouwen, it is never a question of either/or, for it necessitates a balanced cultivation of both. "We all have to find our way home to God in solitude and in community with others" (SD:115), he insists. In this regard, Nouwen sums up well the reciprocal dynamic between solitude and community this way: "Communion with God is where spiritual community begins. Community springs forth from solitude, and without a community, communion with God is impossible" (SD:112;115).

SOLITUDE, COMMUNITY, AND MINISTRY

Henri Nouwen stands convinced that "spiritual formation requires taking not only the *inward journey* to the heart, but also the *outward journey* from the heart to community and ministry" (SF:xxviii). He pinpoints a third vital element of the interactive dynamic between solitude and community by integrating the arena of ministry.

Appealing to Nouwen's progressive schema based on his own analogical interpretation of Luke 6:12–19, we identify a discernible movement from solitude to community to ministry. The order of progression commences with Jesus in communion with God all night long, then calling and gathering his newly formed community around him the following morning so that together they can carry out his commission to do ministry during the afternoon and all through the rest of the day. Symbolically, for Henri Nouwen, *night*, *morning*, and *afternoon* correspond respectively to the sequential flow beginning with *solitude* and on to *community* and climaxing with *ministry*. The kind of formative life

Nouwen considers the true "way of the heart," which can only give way to the real experience of spiritual freedom, calls for such movement "from solitude with God to community with God's people to ministry to and for all" (*SF*:xxvii). Nothing less will do.

Emerging naturally out of this threefold thrust are the three key spiritual practices for our journey, which we all need to cultivate in the most balanced way possible, namely, deepening our communion with God through prayer, strengthening our spiritual bond together as a community, and fulfilling our commission to actively engage in compassionate ministry to the world. While the pattern obviously points to a necessary progression, Nouwen strives to demonstrate how all three—solitude, community, and ministry—also operate within an interactive loop, both reciprocally and cyclically.[3] That, to Nouwen, is what amounts to a fully integrated life in God.

As Nouwen reminds us,

> The God who dwells in our inner sanctuary is also the God who dwells in the inner sanctuary of each human being. Intimacy with God and solidarity with all people are two aspects of the indwelling presence of God. These two realities can never be separated. (*SF*:99)

Self-withdrawal via solitude indeed serves as the foundation for our life together and makes possible the experience of authentic communal engagement. In all practicality, it is the disciplined practice of aloneness that ushers us to deeper connectedness with one another. To put it another way, "Being alone indirectly transforms relationships and builds community" (*CR*:xiv). Our community of faith—whose primary language is prayer—brings our focus back to being in communion with God. As Nouwen puts it, "in prayer we direct ourselves to the one who forms the community" (*RO*:156). The back and forth rhythm of solitude and community maintains and sustains the inseparable dynamic in both of them.

Likewise, we need to be reminded of how *community* and *ministry* are intertwined. Henri Nouwen's view of community has consistently been other-centered versus ingrown. We are gathered for the sake of others. In short, community exists with the service of ministry as its goal—both within and beyond the community.

Our spiritual ministry is decidedly a communal endeavor in that it is directed and employed *in* community, *by* the entire community, *to* the larger community.[4]

Finally, we must also address the crucial interrelationship between *solitude* and *ministry*. As Nouwen puts it, "You cannot *not* minister if you are in communion with God."[5]

"Inner" Spirituality and "Outer" Ministry

Solitude is the hidden venue wherein we deepen our interior life in order to prepare us spiritually to tackle the external demands of a life of ministry. Community becomes the necessary, overarching context for an outwardly focused expression of our ministry. Here both the inward and the outward aspects of our journey explicitly require ongoing interaction. Expounding on what this means more concretely, Nouwen says:

> The journey inward calls for the disciplines of solitude, silence, prayer, meditation, contemplation, and attentiveness to the movements of our heart. The journey outward in community and mission calls for the disciplines of care, compassion, witness, outreach, healing, accountability, and attentiveness to the movement of other people's hearts. These two journeys belong together to strengthen each other and should never be separated. (*SF*:123)

While many of us have often been guilty of separating these journeys, Henri Nouwen has consistently exemplified for us how the various dynamics of *contemplation* and *action*, *prayer* and *service*, the *mystical* and the *prophetic*, to mention a few, ought rather to be construed as conjoined realities. Our so-called interiority and exteriority may function as categorical labels for two dimensions of our lived experience—labels that can prove either helpful or unhelpful—but these dimensions must be held in dialectical tension both conceptually and practically.

We discover in many of Henri Nouwen's writings how he consciously rejected a dualistic perspective on each of these seemingly polar constructs. Evidence abounds as to how he instead actively sought to integrate such polarities under the broad umbrella of *spirituality* and *ministry*—both of which he deemed relationally inseparable as well as indivisible, based upon the Great Commandment.[6] To begin with, Nouwen regarded the Great Commandment—to love God and our neighbor—not as two distinct commands, but equal ones that should never be "made mutually exclusive" nor "substituted one for the other" because, in reality, "all ministry is based on our personal and communal relationship with God" (*LR*:32).

Therefore, Henri Nouwen draws no dividing line between spirituality and ministry. Together they touch and embrace each other within that holy place called solitude, ignited by the dynamic of compassion, which Nouwen identifies as "the fruit of solitude and the basis of all ministry" (*WOH*:26;33). With solitude being the furnace of our inner transformation, a new, converted self emerges from which real compassionate ministry freely flows (*WOH*:20;32). For we can only minister with a true heart of compassion out of a deeply transformed heart permeated by no less than God's compassionate love. Our life then becomes a conduit of overflowing love.

In a truly renewed existence, Nouwen emphasizes, "life itself becomes ministry" where "there is hardly any difference left between doing and being" (*WOH*:37). Aligned with Merton's contemplative vision and conviction, Nouwen is persuaded that "it is in the intimacy with God that we develop a greater intimacy with people" (*LR*:51). By learning to tune in attentively to God's heart more and more, we begin to grow in our capacity to sense God's compassion for the suffering world. Not only are we enabled to grasp, but even more so to experience deep in our hearts, God's love for all flowing through us. Henri Nouwen concludes: "Thus in and through solitude, we do not move away from people. On the contrary, we move close to them through compassionate ministry" (*WOH*:39). Contemplation and action, indeed, go hand in hand.

CONTEMPLATION AND ACTION

"To contemplate is to *see*, and to minister is to *make visible*,"[7] says Nouwen. Thus, "the contemplative life is a life with a vision, and the life of caring for others is a life revealing the vision to others" (*CR*:84). Nouwen explains why and how this "contemplative vision" makes valid sense:

The practice of contemplative prayer is the discipline by which we begin to "see" the living God dwelling in our own hearts. Careful attentiveness to One who makes a home in the privileged center of our being gradually leads to recognition. It is by being awake to this God within that we also find the Presence in the world around us. It is not that we see God in the world, but that God within us recognizes God in the world. (CR:100–101)

What Nouwen refers to as our unique participation in the "divine self-recognition" is that which inspires us toward a more active participation in the life of God's world. No less than God's active presence felt deeply within us can spark such determined action on our part (cf. C:121).

As we are able to access the very heart of God from within the depth of our own hearts through contemplation, we also become empowered to gain access to other people's hearts via compassionate action. Contemplative awareness of this kind can only thrust us beyond ourselves, compelling us to hospitably reach out and minister to others in great need.

Henri Nouwen never thought of contemplation as a requisite for a fruitful ministry. Ministry, as a whole, is about contemplation—"the ongoing unveiling of reality and the revelation of God's light as well as [humanity's] darkness" (CM:63). True contemplation is always active, for it involves constant movement "from opaqueness to transparency, from the place where things are dark, thick, impenetrable and closed to the place where these same things are translucent, open, and offer vision far beyond themselves."[8] Contemplation is action and action is contemplation.

As people who strive to minister more holistically, we are often presented with the challenge of how we can creatively synthesize the simultaneous focus on inwardness and activism. In his book *Creative Ministry*, Nouwen underlines for us their mutual inclusiveness:

Christian life is not a life divided between times for action and times for contemplation. No. Real social action is a way of contemplation, and real contemplation is the core of social action. In the final analysis, action and contemplation are two sides of the same reality which makes a [person] an agent of change. (*CM*:88)

Parker J. Palmer, one of Nouwen's close friends, proposes that instead of talking about contemplation and action, "we might speak of contemplation-and-action, letting the hyphens suggest what our language obscures: that the one cannot exist without the other."[9] Contemplation without action only promotes irrelevant and impotent piety. Action devoid of contemplation leads to unrestrained, de-centered forms of activism. What we need, it seems, is more "contemplated" action and highly "activated" contemplation.

Henri Nouwen often utilized the wagon wheel as a symbol of what it means to conduct a spiritually balanced life—one that is lived out from the center (*HN*:26). The hub or the central axis represents our contemplative center, from which action extends out in the spokes, touching humanity and the world. From this center, we muster the energy to move outside of it. Appealing to this same imagery, author Phileena Heurtz applies it this way:

> Without the center axis, the spokes would lose their anchor and be unable to support the forward motion of the wheel. Without the spokes, the center axis would be deemed extraneous. When we are least connected to our contemplative center, our life is most tense and chaotic. When we are anchored in contemplative spirituality, the active, exterior expression of our life is more peaceful, purposeful, and effective.[10]

What a beautiful way to articulate the practical fusion—as well as the necessary tension—between contemplation and action!

PRAYER AND SERVICE

An even more specific means to illustrate the practical ramifications of the tight interweaving between contemplation and action is through the knitted character of prayer and service, which Henri Nouwen viewed as "*both* expressions of an intimate relationship with God, and through God with all of humanity" (*LS*:52). In and through prayer, we not only recognize our own blessedness but our capacity to bless others as well through serving them (*LB*:63). Nouwen believed that "a life of prayer connects us in the most intimate way with the life of the world"[11] —the same needy world we seek to enter into and serve compassionately.

Prayer and service are never to be looked upon as exclusive of each other. Persuaded of their natural complementarity, Henri Nouwen elaborates on their interactive dynamics:

> If prayer leads us into a deeper unity with the compassionate Christ, it will always give rise to concrete acts of service. And if concrete acts of service do indeed lead us to a deeper solidarity with the poor, the hungry, the sick, the dying, and the oppressed, they will always give rise to prayer. In prayer we meet Christ, and in him all human suffering. In service we meet people, and in them the suffering Christ. (*C*:117)

So intimately connected are they in Nouwen's view that he encapsulates the theme of his book *The Living Reminder* within his conclusive premise that "service is prayer and prayer is service" (*LR*:Back cover).

MYSTICAL AND PROPHETIC

The intimate connection between the mystical and the prophetic thrusts of our journey presents yet another helpful lens through which we can view the unity between our inward spirituality and outward ministry. Henri Nouwen's own practice of mysticism evidenced equal weight placed on both realms. Far from the stereotyped notion of a solitary mystic who is woefully detached from the affairs of the world, Nouwen modeled a mysticism of communal engagement.

Nouwen's norm is very much in keeping with the brand of mysticism that the English contemporary writer, Evelyn Underhill, advocated: a union with the divine that "impels a person toward an active, outside, rather than purely passive, inward life."[12] Upon reading Underhill's *The Mystics of the Church*, Nouwen became even more convinced that "the love of God lived in its fullest sense leads to a most selfless dedication to the neighbor" and that "our intimate union with God leads to the most creative involvement in the contemporary world" (*GD*:177).

Mysticism, therefore, in no way implies passive withdrawal and disengagement from the life of the world. On the contrary, history abundantly attests that "the greatest contemplative figures in the Western spiritual tradition were also people of immense pastoral and prophetic energy."[13] To them, a mystical focus and a prophetic thrust were a joint reality.

In an unqualified sense, "the great mystical truth of the spiritual life," Nouwen stressed, "is that the more intimately connected you are with the Lord, the more in solidarity you are with all the suffering people of the world."[14] He repeatedly insisted that "we cannot live in intimate communion with Jesus without being sent to our brothers and sisters who belong to the same humanity that Jesus has accepted as his own" (LS:45). This shows Nouwen's firm belief in the inherent connection between intimacy and solidarity. Fueled by this conviction, he continually wrestled with the spiritual and social ramifications of the Gospel in many of his writings.[15]

In Jesus, Henri Nouwen reasoned, "the mystical and the revolutionary ways are not opposite ways, but two sides of the same mode of experiential transcendence...Jesus was a revolutionary who did not become an extremist, since he did not offer an ideology but himself. He was also a mystic who did not use his intimate relationship with God to stay away from the social evils of his time" (WH:19–21). Nouwen understood Jesus to be treading the middle ground himself, balancing "a path of activism that speaks truth to those in power while simultaneously remaining grounded in the spiritual qualities of empathy and compassion."[16]

Moreover, for Jesus, "changing the human heart and changing human society are not separate tasks, but are as interconnected as the two beams of the cross" (WH:20). Both are to be seen as coextensive endeavors. Along the same lines, therefore, we may construe mysticism and revolution as "two aspects of the same attempt to bring about radical change" (WH:19).

Philip Sheldrake sums this idea up by declaring that the way we live out our spirituality entails effort at maintaining the proper "dialectic of the mystical and prophetic" because of their necessary complementary roles.[17] As such, both must always be held in constant tension.

Having situated the polarities of solitude and community as the inner/outer dimensions of spirituality and ministry, we are ready to deal more specifically with the ministerial tensions of *compassion/confrontation* and *presence/absence*.

Solitude/Community

FOR PERSONAL REFLECTION

1. How do I venture to find my way home to God through solitude and community? What are some spiritual practices I can cultivate as I travel this path?

2. What would it take for my regular practice of solitude to effect change in my relationship with others and help build community?

3. Why is it vital and necessary to deliberately engage in "contemplated" action and "activated" contemplation? How can I maintain a good balance of these?

Suggested Reflective Exercise

IMAGINATIVE SYMBOLIZATION

Visualize where you see yourself positioned on a continuum between the polarities of *solitude* and *community*. At present, how will you symbolize your own rhythm (or lack of it)?

Next, translate your reflection on paper by drawing your chosen symbol using any medium you are most comfortable with (colored pencil or pen, charcoal, pastel, watercolor, acrylic or oil paint, etc.).

End this simple exercise by offering a prayer prompted by your imaginative portrayal of your current rhythm.

CHAPTER FIVE

Compassion and Confrontation

> Compassion does not exclude confrontation. On the contrary,
> confrontation is an integral part of compassion. Confronta-
> tion can indeed be an authentic expression of compassion.
>
> Henri Nouwen, Compassion

In the previous chapter we saw Henri Nouwen as a person of res-
olute integrity and conviction when it came to managing the tension between the interiority and exteriority of his lived spirituality.
While, to a large extent, much of what was involved in doing so
came much easier for him due to his natural proclivity toward integration, he undoubtedly had to learn certain aspects through indi-
rect as well as firsthand exposure to influential people who had
fleshed out such a balancing act, each in their own way.

Were it not for the "contemplative-active" modeling of key
figures such as Dietrich Bonhoeffer, Martin Luther King, Jr., Jean
Vanier, and Gustavo Gutierrez and the other liberation theologian
advocates, Nouwen's operational spirituality could have remained
heavily slanted toward a more reductionist, individualistic, elitist,
and interiorized version characteristic of the prevailing North
American milieu of his day.[1]

Nouwen consciously avoided falling into this potential trap
by exerting deliberate efforts to be immersed in the reality of

human suffering wherever it might be found. This explains in large part his decision to give up tenure at Yale to explore missionary prospects in Latin America. Deep within him lay a sincere desire to be in solidarity with "the way of the poor, the suffering, the marginal, the prisoners, the refugees, the lonely, the hungry, the dying, the tortured, the homeless—toward all who ask for compassion" (*HN*:101). Nouwen must have imagined this kind of scenario to be an ideal context in which to learn how to exercise compassionate solidarity in deepening ways.

Henri Nouwen's wide-ranging conception of compassionate solidarity, however, is decidedly double-edged. Built into this conception is a confrontational feature. Self-consciously, he proclaims: "In the face of the oppressed I recognize my own face and in the hands of the oppressor I recognize my own hands" (*OH*:56). Nouwen maintains that it is not possible to genuinely profess solidarity with the oppressed apart from our willingness to also confront the oppressor. In addition, confrontation always incorporates self-confrontation—the kind that "prevents us from becoming alienated from the world we confront" (*C*:125). In the words of Thomas Merton, "When I find the world in my own ground, it is impossible to be alienated by it."[2] Nouwen thus unlocks for us the key to this compassionate confrontation:

> The evil that needs to be confronted and fought has an accomplice in the human heart, including our own. Therefore, each attempt to confront evil in the world calls for the realization that there are always two fronts on which the struggle takes place: an outer and an inner front. For confrontation to become and remain compassionate, these fronts should never be separated. (*C*:25–26)

"Compassion without confrontation," he concludes, "fades quickly into fruitless commiseration" (*C*:124).

Compassion seemed to be Henri Nouwen's most natural response to the staggering reality of human suffering—the kind emerging out of an inner solidarity with all of humankind and not out of a self-righteous stance. Compassion takes on an even higher level of significance as the manifestations of suffering are no longer viewed merely as life's unwanted interruptions but as opportunities for transformation—for both ourselves and our fellow humans (*RO:59–60*).

Creative confrontation allows a more holistic process of conversion to take effect in us and in those around us. Insofar as our communal and social duties and responsibilities are concerned, compassionate solidarity side by side with loving confrontation are indeed in order.

Ministry of Caring and Confronting

Beyond our corporate calling to engage in compassionate confrontation with our suffering world, Henri Nouwen saw robust application of this integrated call—in personal and concrete terms—from the ministerial vantage point of administering soul care to people. In particular, Nouwen tangibly demonstrated how the interlocking initiatives of caring and confronting could play out, not just through our efforts to extend hospitality toward others, but even more specifically, as we strive to become sacred companions for others on their spiritual journey.[3]

In line with this, Nouwen spelled out the balanced need for us to choose both "encouragers" and "discouragers" in the guides, counselors, or spiritual directors we look up to:

> We need someone who *encourages* us when we are tempted to give it all up, to forget it all, to just walk away in despair. We need someone who *discourages* us when we move too rashly in unclear directions or hurry proudly to a nebulous goal. (*RO:137*—italics mine)

Too often, we just want to hear what we want to hear, so we are automatically drawn to guides who are quick to validate us. To our disadvantage, we may miss the opportunity of being stretched beyond our own perception of things by not subjecting ourselves to others who can boldly challenge our sometimes myopic or altogether faulty assumptions. All of us possess certain blind spots that require exposure from those who love us enough to confront us. At the same time, the demanding nature of our journey can make it difficult for us to keep pressing forward on our own. We can use spiritual cheerleaders to spur us on when the going becomes rough. We all need to be reminded that it is always too soon to quit just when we are about ready to throw in the towel.

For our own spiritual well-being, we can benefit from both these types of companions who can bring about healthy balance in our lives: affirmers, motivators, and inspirers on one hand; challengers, evaluators, and truth-tellers on the other hand. Similarly, we aspire to be the kind of companion for others who can both freely express loving, compassionate care and be willing and ready to boldly but gently confront when called for.

A split between the two is unwarranted. We can choose to integrate them both, as Jesus—who himself embodied grace and truth—did (see John 1:14, 17). The New Testament shows that Jesus both cared and confronted; he never imposed a dichotomy between love and truth. In fact, he spoke truth in love, which the apostle Paul expects us to imitate (Eph 4:15). The way to minister with both impact and respect is through what is called "care-fronting."[4]

"CARE-FRONTING"

Some three decades ago, pastoral theologian David Augsburger debunked the common practice of treating caring and confronting as distinct and separate by coining the term "care-fronting" in his hugely popular book *Caring Enough to Confront*. Care-fronting appropriately combines "genuine caring that bids another grow" with "real confrontation that calls out new insight and understanding."[5] Augsburger sums his idea up this way:

> Care-fronting unites love and power. Care-fronting unifies concern for relationship with concerns for goals. So one can have something to stand for (goals) as well as someone to stand with (relationship) without sacrificing one for the other, or collapsing one into another. Thus one can love powerfully and be powerfully loving. These are not contradictory. They are complementary.[6]

Henri Nouwen would have had no problem subscribing to this term, for he embodied its essence throughout his ministry.

To those who experienced his companionship on their journey, Henri Nouwen was a sensitively caring and compassionate soul. He ministered with a great deal of authenticity, all the while exemplifying the twin traits of compassion and care, by which he was known to many.[7] Nouwen never distinguished one from the other, as he was convinced that compassion is the *sine qua non* of the true practice of soul care.

Henri Nouwen elaborated: "Care is being with, crying out with, suffering with, feeling with. Care is compassion" (*BJ*:Feb 8). More than the task of curing the soul, Nouwen held that "the care of soul is paramount,"[8] further asserting that to be human is to truly care (*BJ*:Ibid.) and that, essentially, care is the source of all cure.

At L'Arche Daybreak Community, where he spent the last decade of his life ministering to people with mental and physical disabilities, "core members"—as they are called—like David and Gordie poignantly testified how they personally experienced Nouwen's attentive care for their whole well-being.[9] Nouwen's enormous capacity to care deeply for souls is well documented and validated by countless people of diverse backgrounds whose lives he touched profoundly.[10]

As a genuine lover of people, however, Henri Nouwen did not merely reach out to others with compassionate care; he also cared enough to lovingly confront those to whom he ministered—particularly if the truth of any issue was at stake. A case in point is recounted by one of his former spiritual directees, who describes Nouwen's confrontational style: "Henri's intensity has much to do with his relentless interest in the truth...wanting to get you into the truth of who you are. Then he challenges you to move into those inner places where you don't want to go your-self."[11] Nouwen knew just how to enter unhesitatingly and move into people's lives, armed with loving persistence.

No less than his own bosom friend, Nathan Ball, confirms this about Nouwen. Nathan speaks of the manner in which Nouwen directly and unabashedly engaged him, calling him out from his "own place of passivity in relationship to both people and God."[12] Even in their role as co-workers in the same L'Arche community at Daybreak, Nouwen and Nathan managed to mutu-ally "support and challenge each other to provide the kind of lead-ership the community needed."[13] Another very close friend of Nouwen's, Sue Mosteller, gratefully acknowledges how Nouwen gave her a gentle push to take risks at a particularly difficult time while serving at L'Arche. When she felt paralyzed and ready to give it all up, Nouwen was there to both challenge and encourage.[14]

Henri Nouwen was a "care-fronter" in the truest sense of the word. He possessed the knack for combining the tenderness of caring alongside the boldness of confronting others. Effortlessly, he blended all that which many of us often tend to distinguish and separate: love and power, truth and love, grace and truth. Nouwen cared deeply enough to confront, and he confronted with loving care. He further demonstrated this nuanced outworking within the ministry contexts of hospitality and spiritual guidance.

RECEPTIVITY AND CONFRONTATION IN HOSPITALITY

Much has been written on the topic of hospitality and how it figures within the broad umbrella of ministry. Henri Nouwen's unique take on it is hailed by many as the most nuanced, if not the most substantive, in this field of study. The sheer expansiveness of his treatment of the subject is unparalleled, although his conclusion is strikingly plain and simple: Hospitality is ministry and all ministry is hospitality.[15]

Hospitality, Nouwen submits, is not about effecting change in people, but lavishly providing space where such change can actually occur (*RO*:71). Without this crucial element of space, hospitality is less than authentic. As to the categorical meaning of space that he is describing here, Nouwen employs a broad variety of adjectives to qualify what that encompasses: free, friendly, welcoming, open, empty, fearless (*RO*:65ff.). To be sure, Nouwen's ministry of hospitality was empowering. He created space for people to find their own home on their own (cf. *WH*:92; *RO*:72).

How can this type of space be engendered? The hospitable space Henri Nouwen had in mind is all at once inviting, encouraging, trusting, revealing, healing, affirming, compassionate, supportive, and receptive (*RO*:75ff.). He placed particular weight on the importance of receptivity. According to Nouwen, any type of outreach ministry that is lacking in honest receptivity can be dangerous. It can easily give rise to "manipulation and even to violence...in thoughts, words and actions," whereas genuine receptivity has to do with inviting others into our world on their terms, as opposed to ours (*RO*:98). The moment we start imposing our own agenda—including our personal convictions, ideologies, and lifestyle—and use any of that as leverage to determine how far we are willing to connect with others, we slip into exploitative posturing. Hospitality of this sort smacks of a business transaction in which we make sure we have the upper hand (RO:Ibid.). Genuine reception of others—a trademark of hospitality—has love, friendship, and care fueling it, not the manipulative imposition of our viewpoints or attitudes.

Receptivity, however, is but one face of hospitality, as Nouwen presents it; just as critical is the bold face of confrontation. Nouwen explains:

> Real receptivity asks for confrontation because space can only be a welcoming space when there are clear boundaries, and boundaries are limits between which we define our own position. Flexible limits, but limits nonetheless. (RO:Ibid.)

Here Nouwen introduces the need for "articulate presence," which he identifies as "the presence within boundaries," wherein the host assumes a position of "a point of orientation and a frame of reference" for the guest (RO:Ibid.).

Henri Nouwen is obviously balancing the notion that real hospitality is not just about receiving strangers or guests but also confronting them with the kind of presence so direct that it is neither ambiguous nor neutral. Primarily, it means presenting—not imposing—our position to the other in a clear manner:

> No real dialogue is possible between somebody and a nobody. We can enter into communication with the other only when our own life choices, attitudes and viewpoints offer boundaries that challenge the strangers to become aware of their own position and to explore it critically. (RO:99)

Applying this aspect of hospitality directly to our ministry of accompaniment—by coming along with and coming through for somebody on their journey—we need not be timid to bear witness to our convictions so long as we do not impose them on others in a manipulative fashion.

Henri Nouwen was a true example of this attitude and action, according to L'Arche founder Jean Vanier, who said, "[Nouwen] led people closer to Jesus, to truth, to a greater acceptance of themselves and of reality" without ever imposing his own faith on them.[16] He received and accepted others with respect while never failing to be a powerful and continuing witness in their lives.[17]

As Nouwen himself deems it, receptivity and confrontation represent two sides of our Christian witness that we would do well to carefully keep in good balance. He concludes, "Receptivity without confrontation leads to a bland neutrality that serves nobody. Confrontation without receptivity leads to an oppressive aggression which hurts everybody" (RO:Ibid.). Receptivity is a true expression of the tender care that materializes through confrontation.

CONFRONTATION AND INSPIRATION IN GUIDANCE

Henri Nouwen's ministry of spiritual companioning, although vast in scope, can be classified into at least four major areas: spiritual friendship, guidance, mentoring, and spiritual direction.[18] For our purposes here, we will focus on Nouwen's general ministry of guidance.

In one simple but profound sentence, author Deirdre LaNoue captures the outstanding traits of a reliable guide as embodied by Henri Nouwen himself: "The value of a guide is found in his or her ability to meet you where you are, to understand how you got there, and lead you to where you need to be."[19] Nouwen exhibited all these characteristics, as well as others.

In guiding others, Nouwen did not feel compelled to impose his own journeying reality, but met people where they were with utmost respect for the uniqueness of their own spiritual pilgrimage. He showed compassionate understanding and discernment when it came to people's current context and situation. Most of all, he possessed a prophetic vision for those whom he guided, and he was able to articulate that vision with the demeanor of a real "care-fronter" who knew exactly how and when to confront and inspire people along their course. Wendy Greer describes this balanced style of guiding: "As a guide he is definitely a companion on the way, *gently* but *persistently urging* us to seek an ever closer relationship with God."[20]

Henri Nouwen understood guidance to involve "the creation

of space in which the validity of questions does not depend on the availability of answers but on the questions' capacity to open us to new perspectives and horizons" (SD:9). Refusing to be a mere dispenser of answers—like the proverbial theologian who keeps answering questions nobody even asks[21]—Nouwen both challenged and encouraged people to wrestle with their own questions. A former spiritual directee of Nouwen's, Lisa Cataldo, did exactly that. Steeped in her all-or-nothing approach to life, along with her self-imposed black-and-white boundaries, Lisa realized through Nouwen's guiding wisdom that a certain time in our journey is allotted "not for definitive answers but for waiting in the uncomfortable yet necessary place of uncertainty."[22] Learning to live with tough questions without ready answers deepens our faith convictions for it forces us to trust in a God who alone carries all the final answers.

In *The Living Reminder*, Nouwen accentuates the guiding role of a minister as that of employing the two-pronged dynamics of confronting and inspiring. "Confrontation challenges us to confess and repent," he points out, while "inspiration stirs us to look up again with new courage and confidence" (LR:64). Here, Nouwen brings into focus the twin propellants of true change: repentance and faith working hand in hand in a person's life.

Bringing it down to a practical level, Henri Nouwen suggests recovering and maximizing the ministerial art of storytelling when attempting to inspire and confront others, since a story has the inherent quality of being able to create the much-needed space that people always long for in their experience. Nouwen lays out some of the more powerful attributes of a story: "We can dwell in a story, walk around, find our own place. The story confronts but does not oppress; the story inspires but does not manipulate" (LR:66).

Most of us know from experience how stories have a way of catching us off guard, subtly exposing us without inciting resistance. King David's life vividly illustrated this. One only needs to be reminded of the familiar Old Testament account of how Nathan the prophet told a moving tale that paved the way for David's personalized conviction of his sins of adultery and murder (2 Sam 12:1–13). Consequently, this humbling episode occasioned David's eventual composition of Psalm 51—a testimony of his painful but genuine act of repentance, salved only by his renewed faith in a forgiving God.

Henri Nouwen is known to have utilized the proven vehicle of storytelling creatively. In the words of his former colleague from the University of Notre Dame, Peter Naus, "Henri was an excellent storyteller, especially because he had a great sense of drama and perfect timing."[23] By expertly telling timely stories, Nouwen wisely inspired and challenged many of those whom he guided on their spiritual journeys.

Through Henri Nouwen's example, we have seen how the ministerial dynamics of compassion, care, receptivity, and inspiration must be balanced with the ministry of confrontation. Only by consciously merging their co-extensive characters can we manage their built-in tension, while recognizing this as a necessary dialectic to ministering holistically.

◦≼≽◦

Compassion/Confrontation

FOR PERSONAL REFLECTION

1. Why is self-confrontation crucial in cultivating compassionate solidarity? What do I need to recognize about myself in order to better identify with the plight of others?

2. How do I develop "care-fronting" in my ministry to others? What would it necessitate for me to grow in this area?

3. In what tangible ways can I both inspire as well as confront others in their spiritual journey? How can I best harness the creative use of storytelling in this regard?

Suggested Reflective Exercise

"CARE-FRONTATIONAL" POSTURE

Find a quiet corner in which to sit down, completely relaxed. Then gently close your eyes and sit with your two hands resting on your lap in an open palms position. Picture in your mind holding a representative symbol of *compassion* on one hand and *confrontation* on the other hand.

After holding these two symbols separately yet simultaneously for a while, bring your left and right hands together in a folded manner—a prayerful gesture of your desire and intent to integrate "care-frontation" as a lifestyle.

CHAPTER SIX

Presence and Absence

In [Jesus'] absence a new and more intimate presence became possible, a presence which nurtured and sustained...and created the desire to see him again.

Henri Nouwen, *The Living Reminder*

In John's Gospel, we read these words of Jesus forewarning his disciples of his imminent departure from their company: "Nevertheless I tell you the truth: it is to your advantage that I go away, for if I do not go away, the Advocate will not come to you; but if I go, I will send him to you" (John 16:7). Jesus did physically leave his followers on earth just as he foretold, but, as equally promised, he did not abandon them as orphans; he sent his very Spirit to inhabit each of them, thus empowering them to do the task he asked them to do.

The Holy Spirit's dramatic arrival in the disciples' midst on the day of Pentecost, against the backdrop of Jesus' physical absence, serves to highlight an intriguing reality—that of presence in absence. In Jesus' actual absence, he made his own presence felt in a uniquely powerful way through his Spirit.

Authors James and Evelyn Whitehead like to refer to Jesus' absence as a "generous absence," for through the seeming "crisis" the followers of Jesus faced, they themselves emerged as leaders,[1] enabled by the Holy Spirit residing in them. Here we see one operative example of the fascinating dynamics between presence and absence.

From this familiar farewell discourse in the Gospel of John, we can draw several more applications that can have a significant impact on the way we live out our own spirituality and ministry. For one, Henri Nouwen is convinced—insofar as our close relationship with Christ is concerned—that the experience of intimacy deepens through the ongoing interface between presence and absence (*LR*:40). How so? Through the powerful construct of memory.

In verses 13–14 of the same chapter in John, Jesus declares, "When the Spirit of truth comes, he will guide you into all the truth; for he will not speak on his own, but will speak whatever he hears, and he will declare to you the things that are to come. He will glorify me, because he will take what is mine and declare it to you" (John 16:13–14). Here Jesus seems to imply, according to Nouwen, not just the truth that "only in memory will real intimacy with him be possible," but likewise, "only in memory will [the disciples] experience the full meaning of what they have witnessed" (*LR*:41).

We know from the Gospel accounts that the followers of Christ often did not comprehend all that Jesus was about, despite being in close contact with him while he was still on earth. But, as Henri Nouwen points out, a presence more intimate and fresh was made possible by Jesus' absence, the quality of which deeply sustained them amidst their many trying challenges in life. This same unique presence fueled in them an even greater desire to see Jesus physically again (*LR*:42). Nouwen underscores what he perceives as the mysterious interplay between presence and absence in the person of Jesus and how that dynamic directly relates to our own experience of his reality:

> Indeed, it is in Christ's absence that our intimacy with him is so profound that we can say he dwells in us, call him our food and drink, and experience him as the center of our being. (*LR*:Ibid.)

Nowhere is this reality so palpably dramatized with such depth of meaning than in the liturgical celebration of the Eucharist, which stands as a memorial of the death and resurrection of our Lord, one that sustains us in the present time wherein we become cognizant of Jesus' presence in a very real way—even in his actual absence (*LR*:47). In a mystical way, "this early ritual is itself a celebration of presence and absence," since the early believers "recognized that when they broke the bread in Jesus' memory (that is, in his absence), Christ became present to them in ways that enlivened their spirits."[2]

Each time we gather ourselves around the Lord's table with the bread and wine in front of us, we keep encouraging one another with an attitude of gratitude to wait in eager expectation for his coming again. Nouwen adds, "As we affirm his absence we realize that he already is with us" and thus we are able to celebrate Christ's presence in our midst while being reminded of his promises (*LR*:46).

The mystery of God's presence and absence through Jesus Christ—mystifying as it may seem—is not merely an abstract reality. There are in fact rich implications as well as practical ramifications we can extract from this rhythmic interplay, which apply directly to the dynamics of human relationships in general and ministry in particular.

Here Henri Nouwen expounds on the vital importance of engaging in a joint ministry of presence and absence and the necessity of balancing the two. It is one thing to stress the role of each one within the relational context of ministry. It is quite another to hold both in creative tension. Therein lies the bigger challenge: viewing presence and absence beyond their simultaneous and alternating thrusts—that is, grasping the reality of presence in absence and absence in presence.

The Ministry of Presence

No one who seriously and thoughtfully absorbs the writings of Henri Nouwen can help but notice that the notion of presence ranks highest in his overall dynamics of doing ministry. The ministry of presence is not just a given; it is repeatedly emphasized in a variety of different ways in virtually all his works. But Nouwen did not just abundantly address the subject of presence. He lived and breathed out presence, and many of those to whom he reached out validate this in their own experience of him. Michael O'Laughlin echoes what many others say about Nouwen's authentic ministry of presence:

> He gave most people the sense that he was so utterly focused on them that little else mattered, and in most cases, he really was completely tuned in to them. He had an ability to zoom in on the person he was speaking with and block out everything else.[3]

Arguably, presence was the greatest gift Henri Nouwen bestowed upon people. "He was with us," as one of his friends from Yale proudly proclaimed.[4] It is not hard to imagine hearing Nouwen tirelessly reminding one and all—just as he reminded one of those he mentored—that "the ministry is about being present with people."[5] Nothing less counts. Nouwen exercised genuine presence with people because he knew how to be present with himself and his God, who was ever-present to him.

INTEGRATED PRESENCE

In one of his most well-read books, *Reaching Out*, which focuses on the foundations of our spiritual life, Henri Nouwen explicates the idea of presence in an integrated manner, using his schema of the three movements on our journey: toward self, toward others, and toward God. I take liberty in referring to them as the inward, the outward, and the upward (or Godward) movements.

Nouwen identifies three primary disciplines respectively associated with each of these three movements: solitude, hospitality, and prayer. Each of these spiritual practices is designed to help us cultivate real presence inwardly, outwardly, and upwardly. "In solitude we can become present to ourselves," (*RO*:41) or, as Nouwen also puts it, we can be "at home in our own house" (*RO*:101). Only then can we exercise true hospitality toward others and be present for them with the kind of "articulate presence" that only the balance of receptivity and confrontation can engender (*RO*:98–99). It is in prayer, which Nouwen describes as "a loving intimacy with God," that we can be truly present to God, who is present to us and who speaks to us in our solitude

(*RO*:122). From Nouwen's perspective, this quality of real presence comes about through the conscious and deliberate creation of space in our lives.

As I have previously summarized the dynamic outworking of Henri Nouwen's trilogy of real presence, we can thus say:

> In solitude, we become present to ourselves by creating an open space in our heart in order to understand who we truly are in God; through the service of hospitality, we become present with and for others as we create a friendly space wherein we can reach out to them as hospitable soul hosts; by prayer, we become present to the Divine Presence by creating a free space for God so we can understand and experience God more intimately.[6]

Henri Nouwen was able to minister and accompany others on their journey more holistically because he himself learned to cultivate and integrate this threefold intersecting presence—inwardly, outwardly, and upwardly—in his own life.

Nouwen believed that one can only be effectively present for the other if, first of all, one is truly present to one's self and to the God present within the self. As David Benner puts it, "Genuine presence involves being genuinely myself. I can be present for another person only when I dare to be present to myself. And I can be genuinely present to myself only when I can be genuinely present to God."[7] Benner elaborates further:

> We are most open to another when we are also open to our own self. The hospitality we offer ourselves will inevitably determine the limits of the hospitality we are capable of offering others...[B]eing present to one's self is the prerequisite to being available for genuine encounter with other people.[8]

The people whom we seek to accompany by our presence can detect, sooner or later, if we ourselves are disconnected from our own soul and estranged from God, whose very presence we might not feel at all. People experience our love deeply if we love ourselves and let our love for God overflow in and through us. As we grow equally at home with God and ourselves, others will feel increasingly at home with us. This ministry of presence was indeed Henri Nouwen's primary gift to us all!

The Ministry of Absence

While Henri Nouwen emphasizes the ministry of presence as we seek to companion people on their walk with God, he likewise calls for the need to equalize presence with the ministry of absence, which, in his mind, is just as critical to sustain in our ministry (see *IVL*:68). There is definitely room for what Nouwen refers to as "articulate absence"—the exact counterpart of "articulate presence," which we covered in the last chapter.

However, absence, as Nouwen contextualizes it, in no way means not showing up. As he hastens to point out, "without a coming there can be no leaving, and without a presence absence is only emptiness" (*LR*:45). What Nouwen is specifically advocating is a more purposeful art of leaving—an act of "creative withdrawal" (*LR*:44). The rationale for such withdrawal is to pave the way for the Spirit of God to work freely in a person or situation without us potentially getting in the way. In short, "we have to learn to leave so that the Spirit can come" (*LR*:45).

Sometimes our presence, though well meaning, can prove imposing, or at worst, suffocating. If only hospital patients could speak up more truthfully, many of them would probably beg to be left alone for a while instead of being inundated by an endless flow of visitors. Nouwen seeks to expand our customary way of thinking beyond the way we usually operate in our visitation ministry by calling for a sensitive observance of the rhythm of presence and absence. Our coming to be present with others is good but so is our timely departure to ensure that we honor the space that people also need. Absence can provide some breathing room for people to come to terms with themselves or their situation on their own apart from our presence, which may be stifling at times.

Nouwen is persuaded that "there is a ministry in which our leaving creates space for God's spirit and in which, by our absence, God can become present in a new way" (*LR*:44). Being in complete step with the Spirit requires that we be discerning as to how God chooses to work in people and certain circumstances, so that we do not end up becoming a hindrance to God's way.

There are times when appropriate withdrawal or backing off from a situation or individual may be the best way to cooperate with God's intentions. To do otherwise can potentially abort the process as well as the timing of God's unique work in people's lives.

Our tendency to eagerly come to people's rescue when they seem to be in dire need—and even our sometimes premature acts of offering comfort or consolation when we can no longer stand the sight of their suffering—can actually get in the way of what God may be doing inside their hearts. Though our withdrawal may not convey the surface appearance of love and concern, sometimes the truly loving thing to do is to back off for a while and resist the temptation to play God by trying to fix others and their seemingly messy circumstances.

Without our willingness and readiness to exercise this art of creative withdrawal, we can easily find ourselves "in danger of no longer being the way, but *in* the way; of no longer speaking and acting in his name, but in ours; of no longer pointing to the Lord who sustains, but only to our own distracting personalities" (*LR*:47–48). However, when we learn how to incorporate this purposeful, articulate absence in our ministry, we are afforded the meaningful opportunity to "participate in the leaving of Christ, the good leaving that allows the sustaining Spirit to come" (*LR*:48).

Nouwen points out our all-too-common tendency to be over-available, which he associates with our desire to feel needed. This can lead us into setting ourselves up as indispensable creatures— a deceptive illusion that we need to shatter each time we become conscious of it (*LR*:49). The God-complex in us can readily take over if we fail to rein in our fleshly drive to act like the savior we are not. Only Jesus can fully come through for people.

Yet even Jesus did not come through for everyone to whom he sought to minister. If we examine the Gospel accounts, we discover that Jesus himself was not always available for people. Neither did he feel compelled to be so, despite the expectations imposed upon him, even by those closest to him. Just imagine the pained words his friend Martha uttered when he finally came to see her brother Lazarus who had just died, "Lord, if you had been here, my brother would not have died" (John 11:32b). Jesus did not predictably heal everyone or perform miracles on demand. He had his own reasons for choosing to be unavailable. In the case of Lazarus, he revealed to his disciples what was behind his seemingly delayed action: "Then Jesus told them plainly, 'Lazarus is dead. For your sake I am glad I was not there, so that you may believe. But let us go to him'" (John 11:14). Jesus knew how and when to be present and absent, as dictated by his divine purposes, which were infinitely higher than our human expectations.

In the midst of his active ministry, Jesus consistently pulled away from people. But as Henri Nouwen qualifies, when Jesus did so, it was always for the purpose of being with his Father (*LR*:50). Indeed, he "continued to return to hidden places to be alone with God," to be nourished through prayer (*BJ*:Aug 13). To be sure, it was a calculated, purposeful withdrawal.

Henri Nouwen believed that there is a particular sense of unavailability that is vital for the minister's spiritual well-being. This is so in order that the minister can devote unhurried time to prayer, which he deemed as reason enough to be creatively unavailable (*LR*:49). He gives the following example:

> When someone says, "The minister is unavailable because this is his day of solitude…could that not be a consoling ministry? What it says is that the minister is unavailable to me, not because he is more available to others, but because he is with God, and God alone—the God who is our God. (*LR*:49)

As Nouwen concludes, "When our absence from people means a special presence to God, then that absence becomes a sustaining absence" (*LR*:50).

Presence in Absence and Absence in Presence

The dynamics of presence and absence, when creatively applied within the realm of human relationships, generate a vision of intimacy much like the fascinating art of dancing where a right balance between closeness and distance is required. Henri Nouwen applies the artful maneuverings of dancers this way: "Sometimes we are very close, touching each other or holding each other; sometimes we move away from each other and let the space between us become an area where we can freely move" (*BJ*:Feb 22). This intentional balancing requires hard work on our part if we wish to participate in the dance of life in a more life-giving way.

Particularly within the context of ministry, our presence—via the powerful avenue of memory—can be experienced more appreciatively by others through creative gestures of absence on our part. As Henri Nouwen qualifies it, there is a certain kind of absence that yields an abiding presence for "if we are able to be fully present to our friends when we are with them, our absence too will bear many fruits," paving the way for them to "discover in our absence the lasting grace of our presence" (BJ:Mar 13).

Likewise, through our absence, there can be a much more compelling presence felt through the unhindered work of the Spirit while we deliberately engage in prayer on behalf of those with whom we cannot be literally present at particular junctures in their journey. Henri Nouwen may be right in pointing out that, more often than not, the Spirit of God reveals himself more distinctly during the course of our absence—usually during those nonorchestrated moments when we are not likely to give in to the urge of wanting to help God out. Nouwen assures us:

> When we claim for ourselves that we come to our friends in the name of Jesus—that through us Jesus becomes present to them—we can trust that our leaving will also bring them the Spirit of Jesus. Thus, not only our presence but also our absence becomes a gift to others. (BJ:Mar 14)

With his characteristic flair for organizing his thoughts into three main points, Henri Nouwen summarizes his own conclusions about the dialectic between the ministry of presence and the ministry of absence:

- We sustain each other in the constant interplay between absence and presence.

- A sustaining ministry asks ministers to be not only creatively present but creatively absent.

- A creative absence challenges ministers to develop an ever-growing intimacy with God in prayer and to make that the source of their entire ministry. (LR:53)

The ministries of presence and absence represent spiritual polarities that can be employed both alternately and simultaneously in a cooperative mode, despite their inherent tension. Henri Nouwen has proven that this is both possible and necessary as we seek to embody a more authentic and well-integrated spirituality of ministry.

Parts I and II dealt with the inward and outward tensions in our journey, corresponding respectively with the psychological and ministerial dynamics. Part III focuses on the upward tensions, along with their corresponding theological dynamics. Here we confront the last three sets of polarities: suffering/glory, present/future, and life/death.

Presence/Absence

FOR PERSONAL REFLECTION

1. Can I identify the various ways I am tempted to be "in the way" rather than pointing others "to the way" as I minister to people?

2. What makes it difficult for me to exercise "creative withdrawal" in my ministry? How can I be fully "unavailable" to others when it is necessary?

3. In caring for people, how can I sustain felt presence amidst my physical absence?

Suggested Reflective Exercise

POLARITY LECTIO

Engage in a private lectio (*Read, Reflect, Respond, Rest*), alternating between two suggested passages that highlight Jesus' abiding presence (Matt 28:20b) and his physical absence (John 16:7).

Then pray how you can personally apply what you have gleaned from this "polarity lectio" exercise. More specifically, try to reflect on how you can creatively "incarnate" (flesh out or live out) these two contemporaneous realities of presence and absence in your ministry to others.

Ask yourself: What would it mean for me to "go away" and yet to "always be with" others whom I am seeking to accompany on their journey?

PART III

Living with *Upward* Polarities
(Theological Tensions)

Jesus calls us to recognize that gladness and sadness are never separate, that joy and sorrow really belong together, and that mourning and dancing are part of the same movement.

Henri Nouwen, *Spiritual Formation*

CHAPTER SEVEN

Suffering and Glory

Let's always look at Jesus, because in his crucified and glorified heart we will see ourselves called to share in his suffering as well as in his glory.

Henri Nouwen, *Bread for the Journey*

The Lord Jesus in the Bible is simultaneously portrayed as the suffering Christ—"a man of suffering and acquainted with infirmity" (Isa 53:3)—and the glorified Christ who had always possessed God's glory even before the creation of the world (John 17:24). As believers in Christ, we mirror this portrait as we are called upon to share in both his suffering and his glory. No less than the apostle Paul expresses this calling to be his uppermost ambition: "I want to know Christ and the power of his resurrection and the sharing of his sufferings by becoming like him in his death" (Phil 3:10). Like Paul's, our spiritual life is destined to embody the tension between these two equal yet seemingly contrasting goals: to experience the reality of Christ's resurrection power and glory as well as to participate fully in his sufferings.

Henri Nouwen assures us that if we truly seek to follow Jesus and begin living seriously in consonance with our real status as joint heirs with him (Rom 8:17), "we will not only come to know the full freedom of the children of God but also the full rejection of the world," sharing in the "full honor as well as the full pain of the Christian life." Best of all, so long as "we are willing to share in the suffering of Christ, we too will share in his glory" (*BJ*:June 6).

Paul, who counts the experience of ongoing suffering—especially suffering for Christ—as a mighty privilege, also speaks about the ever-increasing glory that is ours to claim as we allow God's Spirit to continually perform his transforming work in and through us (2 Cor 3:18). As Nouwen paraphrases Paul, "All of us, with unveiled faces like mirrors reflecting the glory of the Lord, are being transformed into the image that we reflect in brighter and brighter glory" (*BJ*:Nov 11).

As we commune with God, appropriating what Henri Nouwen calls "the prayer of the heart," we can recognize more clearly that our intimate union with God—which is essentially what communion is—involves the God of suffering and the God of glory. Nouwen drives this case home through his recounting of the two specific instances in which Jesus summoned his inner circle of friends—Peter, James, and John—to accompany him as he engaged his Father in communing prayer:

> The first time he took them to the top of Mount Tabor, and there they saw his face shining like the sun and his clothes white as light (Matthew 17:2). The second time he took them to the garden of Gethsemane, and there they saw his face in anguish and his sweat falling to the ground like great drops of blood (Luke 22:44). The prayer of the heart brings us both to Tabor and Gethsemane. When we have seen God in his glory we will also see him in his misery, and when we have felt the ugliness of his humiliation we also will experience the beauty of his transfiguration. (*RO*:150)

Suffering and glory are intimately bound together in our spiritual experience, just as they were for Jesus himself. How exactly do they entwine and correlate? What sparks the tension between them?

Suffering Our Way into Glory

In some sense we can partake in the reality of freedom and glory in the here and now, amidst our varied experience of suffering: "Where the Spirit of the Lord is, there is freedom" (2 Cor 3:17). From Henri Nouwen's perspective, "we are the glory of

God when we give full visibility to the freedom of the children of God" (*BJ*:June 18; see Rom 8:16). Paul himself points out that this is possible through the agency of the Holy Spirit conforming us into Christ's own image from glory to glory.

Still, due to the pervasive presence of sin that is yet to be fully eradicated in our lives, we are bound to keep falling short of God's glory (Rom 3:23). As such, glory, in its fullest sense, will always remain a future reality. Theologians generally refer to this as the state of our final glorification, which will take place when we meet Jesus face to face and become instantly transformed into his likeness.

In the meantime, we patiently march our way through our journey, allowing the inner experience of transformation to occur incrementally—from one degree of glory to another—even in the middle of suffering. Suffering becomes the means and the gateway to complete glory. In this life, our greatest conformity to Christ comes out of the furnace of suffering. Paul implies that it is more in accordance with the pattern of Christ's death, rather than his resurrection glory, that we actually experience our present, ongoing transformation (Phil 3:10–11).

When Jesus raised the penetrating question before the two brothers James and John, "Can you drink the cup that I am going to drink?" (Matt 20:22b)—with direct reference to the ultimate suffering to which he would be subjected on the cross—he strongly implied to both of them that "suffering was the only and necessary way to glory" (CYD:48–49). Jesus reinforced this same conviction when he asked the two disciples walking on the road to Emmaus: "'Was it not necessary that the Christ should suffer before entering into glory?' [Luke 24:26]" (CYD:49).

In his letter to the Romans, Paul echoes this fundamental correlation between suffering and glory from the divine perspective: "It is that very Spirit bearing witness with our spirit that we are children of God, and if children, then heirs, heirs of God and joint heirs with Christ—if, in fact, we suffer with him so that we may also be glorified with him" (Rom 8:16–17). Contrasting our present suffering with future glory, Paul exclaims, "I consider that the sufferings of this present time are not worth comparing with the glory about to be revealed to us" (Rom 8:18). Elsewhere, the apostle further expresses a related truth that we would do well to be reminded of constantly: "For this slight momentary affliction is preparing us for an eternal weight of glory beyond all measure" (2 Cor 4:17).

In God's grand scheme of things, suffering and glory are necessarily linked. In applying this to the metaphorical notion of "drinking the cup of life," Henri Nouwen discloses to us that "our cup of sorrow is also our cup of joy and that one day we will be able to taste the joy as fully as we now taste the sorrow" (CYD:49). When we begin to realize more fully that the two cups cannot be separated—that "joys are hidden in sorrows"—then we are more ready to partake of the cup of life and drink it willingly (CYD:50–51).

OUR HOPE OF GLORY

Keeping in mind that there is indeed a glorious day waiting for us on the horizon stirs up a live hope inside of us in spite of the fact that we are bound to suffer our way into glory. The truth is, it is our willing engagement with suffering that slowly but surely gives rise to our hope of glory. Henri Nouwen affirms the reality of such hope, stating: "It is in this mystery of union in suffering that hope is hidden" (WJ:29). Essentially, this is what the apostle Paul reveals as "the riches of the glory of this mystery, which is Christ in [us], the hope of glory" (Col 1:27b).

True, the tension is so real because we will continue wrestling in our hearts about the incompleteness of what we ultimately long for, even though we are already given a foretaste of it. All of us deeply desire now that which God has fully reserved for the future. Yet hope is just as real, as Henri Nouwen keeps stressing to us. We can live with and in hope: "the trust that God will fulfill God's promises to us in a way that leads us to true freedom" (BJ:Jan 16).

What keeps this hope alive and burning within us is the sustaining presence of the Holy Spirit, who jointly bears witness with our spirits that we truly belong to God (see Rom 8:16). The Scripture tells us that the Spirit is given to us as a deposit, guaranteeing our full inheritance that is yet to come (2 Cor 1:22). John, the Beloved, writes, "Dear friends, now we are children of God, and what we will be has not yet been made known. But we know that when he appears, we shall be like him, for we shall see him as he is. Everyone who has this hope in him purifies himself, just as he is pure" (1 John 3:2–3). Hope serves as our empowerment for a life of holiness—hope that is "forward looking and forward moving, and therefore also revolutionizing and transforming the present."[1]

Hope, however, does not eliminate the existence of tension. The dynamics of tension and hope will continue to play out as we live our life in Christ, immersed as we all are in our core struggle: the simultaneous realities of battle and victory.

Battle and Victory

The true nature of our life with God on this side of heaven has always been—and will most likely continue to be—the subject of much speculation and debate. Far from being a settled issue, the perennial question of what constitutes the so-called normal Christian life still seems to plague us, and no answer appears satisfactory to put it to rest. In revisiting this question, perhaps it might be worth pondering whether we are asking the right question to begin with. Is there really such a thing as *the* "normal" Christian life?

The usually rigid answers supplied to this question only serve to showcase how skewed our prevailing thinking is. There is sharp division and strong opinion on this issue. At whichever extreme we may find ourselves, each betrays our natural propensity toward an "either/or" mindset. Generally speaking, we run into two theological camps, each espousing its own definitive stance: one that takes a dim or defeatist view and another that advocates a triumphal read on the outworking of our Christian life.

Based largely on the intense internal battle experienced by every believer as portrayed by Paul in Romans 7, the first camp concludes that our spiritual life can only be realistically typified by a life of ongoing struggle. With the insidious presence of the "flesh" continuing to rear its ugly head, we are bound to wrestle our way through our entire Christian life until we breathe our last breath. Struggle is viewed as a norm for which there is no complete solution in sight—at least not while we are still in our earthly dwelling.

On the other side, we find those who appeal to the truth that Paul articulates in Romans 8, exalting the victory we can claim through the empowerment of the Holy Spirit dwelling within us. This group submits that our spiritual life ideally is meant to be one of sustained, moment-by-moment victory over the power of sin in our lives. A life of victory is the standard; anything less is substandard, or worse, abnormal.

Which of these views correctly represents the real nature of our life with God? Truth be told, neither of them—that is, if we insist on totally separating the two chapters of Romans that these camps use to bolster their extreme positions and setting them against each other, as do many who assume that Romans 7 and 8 must be purely antithetical to each other.

In a limited way, Romans 7 pictures for us a somewhat realistic but never the most ideal representation of our spiritual journey, while Romans 8, also in an limited fashion, gives us a glimpse of the ideal yet real portrayal of what our life with God should be about. We know quite painfully, from experience, that we will continuously struggle to maintain our newfound freedom in Christ in our daily life. At the same time, we are gloriously aware of the Spirit's power, which enables us to experience true spiritual freedom in the here and now.[2]

However, a more integrated interpretation of Romans 7 and 8 allows us to grasp these two seemingly opposing realities as coexistent—like viewing them as two sides of the same coin. Biblical scholar C. E. B. Cranfield is right in upholding the need for us to "resolutely hold chapters 7 and 8 together, in spite of the obvious tension between them, and see in them not two successive stages but two different aspects, two contemporaneous realities, of the Christian life."[3]

The experience of freedom and victory highlighted by Paul in Romans 8 can only be meaningfully appreciated against the backdrop of the ever-mounting struggle depicted earlier in Romans 7. For it is certain that one can struggle without gaining victory, but one cannot possess true victory apart from real struggle. Henri Nouwen recognized this when he said, "Spiritual freedom requires a fierce spiritual battle" (*IVL*:xix). Nouwen sees this as a genuine battle: "the battle is real...you will only know what victory is when you have been part of the battle" (*GD*:71–72). Battle and victory do go hand in hand and must never be treated as though they are distinctly separate phenomena.

Our ongoing spiritual battle is best viewed as a prelude to the complete victory and deliverance that await us—in much the same way that the present suffering we encounter is regarded as the preliminary route to glory. Henri Nouwen, however, exposes the tendency of many of us to shortcut this process because "we...like easy victories: growth without crisis, healing without pains, the resurrection without the cross."[4]

Nonetheless, the inescapable conclusion we arrive at is that while every experience of triumph, victory, deliverance, freedom, healing, joy, or glory in our present time can be genuine and real, it is by no means total and complete. For as long as we are not yet home in glory, everything is partial. In C. S. Lewis's words, "nothing is yet in its true form."[5] Thus our struggle mounts up because "we have a heart that desires things that are complete, and we live—always—in situations that can seem only incomplete."[6] Although it is hard for us to accept such a reality, we must learn to live with it, knowing that, in the consummation of things, everything will be brought to its grand completion.

Meanwhile, tension and hope will surely continue to commingle in all of our experience, due in large part to the inevitable overlap between the equal realities of the present and the future, to which we turn in the following chapter.

⚜

Suffering/Glory

FOR PERSONAL REFLECTION

1. As I reflect upon my own journey, can I identify a certain period or event where I experienced a simultaneous sense of suffering and God's transforming glory? What feelings and/or insights do I recall from such an experience?

2. What does it mean for me personally to be conformed to Christ in the here and now according to the pattern of his death? What will it take for me to enter into this process openly?

3. How can I live both with hope and in hope amidst the tensional reality of suffering and glory in our world?

Suggested Reflective Exercise

OBJECT REMINDER

Pick a special coin that you can carry around in your purse or pocket. Or you may wish to put it in a visible place in your home or office. Each time you touch it or pull it out, let this object bring to mind the notion that *suffering* and *glory* as well as *battle* and *victory* are akin to different sides of the same coin.

Such an object can serve as a gentle reminder that both sides represent equal realities that must be lived in tension. Each time you feel the coin, you can choose to openly embrace the experience of tension in your journey and prayerfully claim its transformative value.

You may wish to engage in this exercise time and again.

CHAPTER EIGHT

Present and Future

The marvelous vision of the…Kingdom…calls for its realization in our day-to-day lives. Our visions enable us to live
the full life.

Henri Nouwen, *Bread for the Journey*

From a strictly human standpoint, the present and the future are
normally taken to be as far apart as they can be from each other,
and any possibility of intersection between them is hardly enter-
tained as even an option. When, for some reason, the present gets
mixed in with the future and vice versa, a certain feeling of tension builds up and upsets our sense of equilibrium.

As far as the present and the future are concerned, we would
much rather draw a solid line between them so we can deal with
each of them accordingly—or separately. We prefer the division to
be neat and tidy, not blurry. We want to stick with the present or
the future but never with both at the same time. Predictably, our
sense of control over our life is at issue.

Within the realm of the spiritual, however, the demarcation
we insist on establishing may not appear as clear-cut as we expect
or imagine. The present can get enmeshed with the future and the
future can seem to invade the present. Henri Nouwen says: "For
anyone who has listened deeply to the heart of God, the despair
of the world and the coming of the great liberation are both visible every day" (*BJ*:Sept 17). As we are about to see, this is one of

the conundrums of our spiritual journey—which itself is far from linear; rather, it is often circular, cyclical, spiral, or even seasonal. In fact, we can even experience its reality in overlapping ways.

The Overlap of the Ages

We do not find it strange when we experience a certain season overlapping with the next one—whether it be winter, spring, summer, or fall. So why should we be baffled by the same phenomenon in spiritual "ages," such as the overlap between the new age that is yet to come and the old age that is already fading out?

This is precisely the genius behind Paul's theology. All of us are caught up in this so-called "overlap of the ages," since the future has already broken into our present.[1] New life has been inaugurated such that those of us who are still very much a part of this present world are now trying to live as though already belonging to the world that is yet to come. Simply stated, we are engaged in "living the life of the new age in the old age."[2]

TENSION IN THE OVERLAP

The tensional dynamic associated with the overlap of the ages is essentially a theological one. In saying so, I am in no way implying that it is emptied of anything practical. That would go against Henri Nouwen's construal of what true theology is—which is inherently practical and experiential. It is reckoned as theological because the very concept emanates from above, from the very mind of God, thus bleeding with undercurrents of mystery.

While a new life of freedom is real for those of us patently identified with the new age, it remains incomplete until the day we finally exit from the old age, in which we are still caught up. What we experience is but "a foretaste of the new age and the first fruits of its blessings, not the blessings in full."[3] The indwelling presence of the Holy Spirit in us constitutes the first fruits—the pledge of ultimate victory but not yet the fullness of the age to come. To use one theologian's well-crafted phrase, the Holy Spirit is "evidence of the 'presence of the future'" and at the same time signals "the beginning of the end."[4]

In several of the apostle Paul's stated motivations for Christian living, there exists a corollary tension between what theologians refer to as the *indicative* and the *imperative* aspects of our spiritual life. George Eldon Ladd explains how we can best understand their interplay:

> The indicative involves the affirmation of what God has done to inaugurate the new age; the imperative involves the exhortation to live out this new life in the setting of the old world. The new is not wholly spontaneous and irresistible. It exists in a dialectical tension with the old. Therefore the simple indicative is not enough; there must always be the imperative.[5]

Merely assenting to the truth of our new life, as indicated by the entrance of the new age, will not make much difference until we heed the imperative to make a conscious effort to live out that new life, albeit within the context of the old age.

To bring in a related perspective, we can also conceive of the tension as arising from the uncomfortable situation of being suspended, as it were, between the cross and the resurrection. This is so despite the fact that Christ's "resurrection life casts its shadow into the present."[6] When Jesus appeared to the disciples in his resurrected body, they knew he was no longer part of their own world. But, as Henri Nouwen points out, it was precisely this encounter with the resurrected Christ that assured the disciples of the resurrection life that they too will experience someday (*BJ*:Dec 1). In other words, their experience hinted at the promised new life that was now available for them—as it is for all of us as well. Interestingly, living our new life in the old age is akin to the tension of trying to live out Easter reality in a Good Friday world.[7] As if this were not enough, a related, though much more encompassing, tension further beleaguers us.

The "Now" and the "Not-Yet"

The existential overlap of the ages between the new and the old spreads a wider umbrella of tension, which New Testament scholar James Dunn identifies as "the tension between a work 'begun' but not yet 'complete,' between fulfillment and consummation, between a decisive 'already' and still to be worked out 'not yet.'"[8] The heart of the tension lies between the *already* inaugurated and not yet consummated eschatology in our spiritual experience.

Theologian David Dockery stresses that our "life in the Spirit is to be lived out between the polarities of what has been accomplished by the historical achievement of Jesus and what is yet to be fully realized in the consummation of God's redemptive program."[9] Therefore, for the time being, all of us will grapple, at least temporarily, with such tension.

But in many ways, it is a good and healthy kind of tension in that our own spiritual growth gets hastened in the midst of it. As we flesh out the practical realities of "the already and the not yet," we get to exercise patience and hope in God. Such a context of growth, Henri Nouwen reassures us, can sustain us even as we courageously wrestle with having "to live for a while with the 'not yet,'" aware of the fact that our "deepest, truest self is not yet home" (IVL:50).

HOPE AMIDST TENSION

We are all brought face to face with the realization that "the tension with all its real anguish and also all its real hopefulness, [is one] in which the Christian never ceases to be involved so long as he [or she] is living this present life."[10] Note, however, that the tension itself is coupled with the indispensable dynamic of hope. Such a dynamic is more than enough to energize us to keep going, regardless of tough challenges we encounter along the way. Inside we possess a confidence and assurance that there is a glorious climax at the end of our life's journey. We do have hope we can embrace—a strong and active kind with sure expectation of fulfillment.

Henri Nouwen declares, "It is this joyful expectation of God's coming that offers vitality to our lives," and it is the "expectation of the fulfillment of God's promises to us [that] allows us to pay full attention to the road on which we are walking" (BJ:Nov 21). Nouwen wants to plant into our deepest consciousness the inspiring reality that while our journey home is a lifelong process, our Lord Jesus accompanies us along the road, talking to us, and as we listen attentively we realize that, in a sense, "we are already home while on the way" (BJ:Jul 1).

There is something rewarding about keeping our eyes focused on Jesus, as the author of the book of Hebrews admonishes us, because as we do so, we are able to endure our way through his consoling presence as the "pioneer and perfecter of our faith." This is the same Jesus, "who for the sake of the joy that was set before him endured the cross, disregarding its shame, and has taken his seat at the right hand of the throne of God" (Heb 12:2). We too can have the foretaste of joy as we set high our own expectation of him.

"When we have the Lord to look forward to, we can already experience him in the waiting," Nouwen says (*BJ*:Nov 23). Such patient and expectant waiting, according to him, is "full of joy since in prayer we already see the glory of him we are waiting for" (*RO*:151). Our expectation is never vacuous. True, it is tension-filled, but it is likewise hope-filled.

Henri Nouwen beautifully expounds on the mysterious but nonetheless comforting outworking of the "now and the not-yet" as follows:

> The paradox of expectation is that those who believe in tomorrow can better live today; those who expect joy to come out of sadness can discover the beginnings of a new life amid the old; those who look forward to the returning Lord can discover him already in their midst.[11]

A paradox indeed! Yet in Henri Nouwen's unique way of conceptualizing—which, to him, always functions as "an integrating matrix"—paradoxes are normatively expressed as "lived reality."[12] Thus, Nouwen can verbalize the following with a dose of realism only he can convey: "I am still waiting, yet already receiving; still hoping, yet already possessing; still wondering, yet already knowing" (*IM*:62).

All things considered, worldly reality continues to stare us in the eye each waking moment, reminding us constantly what one writer has well summed up for us: "For the moment, though, we are still on the road. The gap between promise and performance is still the tension of our faith. Yet hope is the most compelling incentive in the world."[13]

DYNAMIC OF HOPE

It is true that in this present time, we live in tension—but one that we know will one day be resolved. Against this very tension, the overwhelming reality of hope shines more brightly. The glory looming on the horizon—which is at once incomparable, weighty, and eternal—never ceases to fuel hope's energy, thus transforming and enlivening our vision both of the present and of the future. Henri Nouwen insists that as we anticipate "the marvelous vision of the peaceable Kingdom," this kingdom makes demands for its actualization in our everyday lives (*BJ*:Dec 13). This we need to remember often, for as long as we keep this perspective in mind, "we will find new energy to live it out, right where we are," so that "instead of making us escape real life, this beautiful vision gets us involved" (*BJ*:Ibid.). Not only does it energize us from the inside and out, but it enables us to live life to the fullest (*BJ*: Dec 12).

Our grand homecoming, representing God's crowning vision of his redemptive work in and through Christ, as Nouwen pictures it, is cosmic in scope. The whole of creation will share in our full freedom as God's children. In the final end, all of God's creation will be lifted up into His glory (*BJ*:Dec 8). Hope, by then, will have turned into complete reality!

For now, we must seek to live our lives to the fullest with the intent of learning how to befriend the realities of both life and death, light and darkness, joy and sorrow. This is a fitting conclusion to our attempts to confront the various polarities of our spiritual living. The dialectic between life and death remains the pinnacle of tension in our journey.

⚮

Present/Future

FOR PERSONAL REFLECTION

1. What would be required of me in order to more courageously wrestle with the tension between "the now and the not-yet" experience of life?

2. How can I keep allowing hope to float in the thick of ever-mounting challenges I constantly face? What difference, if any, does that make in my life?

3. Why is it important for me to keep the vision of the kingdom at the forefront? What can I do in the here and now to nurture this vision?

Suggested Reflective Exercise

HOPE AMIDST LONGING

In our spiritual experience, the future no doubt intersects with the present and the present with the future in what theologians famously label as "the already and the not-yet" phenomenon. Pausing to ponder this reality, try to draw from your heart some answers to these questions:

1. Identify at least three things from your own experience that strengthen and sustain your sense of hope at the present moment.

2. Name at least three of the deepest longings of your heart that you envision to be fully realized in the future.

Pay attention to the tension you may be feeling while answering these questions. Breathe *in* your present hope and breathe *out* your future longing (and vice versa).

CHAPTER NINE

Life and Death

Precisely as we confront life and death in all its many facets,
we can finally say to God: "I love you too."
Henri Nouwen, *Spiritual Formation*

In his personal memoir *The Gift of Peace*, Joseph Cardinal
Bernardin, a longtime friend of Henri Nouwen's, recalled how
Nouwen struck him as a person of preparedness who "spent a
lifetime teaching others how to live, and how to die."[1] There is no
doubt that Henri Nouwen not only loved life and lived a very full
life; he also was unafraid to die, and seemed ready and prepared
for death's eventuality. Matters of life and death—with all the
unknowns that go with their territory—did not seem to be a particularly vexing issue for Nouwen. Once he remarked, "If life is a
mystery, why should death be viewed as reality within our grasp
and understanding?" (*IM*:22).

What concerned Nouwen the most was "to live and to die in
gratitude."[2] With a generally positive outlook, Nouwen did live and
die an immensely grateful person, as many of his closest friends can
attest. He never seemed preoccupied with the obvious polarities
between life and death. Unlike the common tendency of many of us
to sharply dichotomize their imposing—and opposing—realities,
Henri Nouwen instead learned how to befriend them both over time.

Nouwen always believed in the need for us to consistently
welcome the totality of our experiences and be "empowered to

embrace all that life brings," since we all are participants in the life, death, and resurrection of Jesus.[3] This perspective displays the widely inclusive mindset out of which Nouwen learned to operate. Ultimately, how we manage to conduct our existence depends a great deal upon the way we view life and death, including the meanings we assign to each. Nouwen sets forth the value and significance of their interconnection: "Life is a school in which we are trained to depart."[4] Here, Nouwen is touching "the great paradox in life: to live in order to be able to die" (LC:49).

Picturing a newborn baby, as well as an old person dying, lets us recall not only how precious life is but also how strikingly "life and death are connected by vulnerability" (BJ:Jan 3). Both require "care, attention, guidance, and support" to make them the meaningful realities that they actually are and should be (BJ:Ibid.). Both need to be celebrated at various times and occasions as deemed appropriate.

"Celebration," according to Henri Nouwen, "is only possible through the deep realization that life and death are never found completely separate," and that "fear and love, joy and sorrow, tears and smiles can exist together" (CM:91). Life and death never fail to interact continuously, whether we like it or not, and whether or not we are even conscious of it. Nouwen goes on to explain that

> ...those who are able to celebrate life can prevent the temptation to search for clean joy or clean sorrow. Life is not wrapped in cellophane and protected against all infections...When we have been able to celebrate life in all these decisive moments where gaining and losing—that is, life and death—touched each other all the time, we will be able to celebrate even our own dying because we have learned from life that the one who loses it can find it (cf. Matthew 16:25).[5]

Jesus offers a radical vision of reality that stands in stark contrast to the worldly one. Nouwen points to the cross as the most potent symbol of this new vision: "a symbol of death *and* of life, of suffering *and* joy, of defeat *and* of victory"—showing us the way and leading us on (HN:39).

Befriending and Celebrating Life

Many people can spend a lifetime without giving any serious thought to the true essence of life; life passes by almost unnoticed for them. To be disconnected from life itself can truly be a sad affair. We may forget what Henri Nouwen consistently affirms, that "it belongs to the essence of being human that we contemplate our life" and that "the greatest joy as well as the greatest pain of living come not only from what we live but even more from how we think and feel about what we are living" (CYD:26). Life without reflection does not amount to much, because as human beings we are wired to be meaning-seeking creatures whose urge for sense-making at times goes far deeper than our need for physical survival.

Drinking the cup of our lives—to use of one of Nouwen's favorite metaphors inspired by his faithful devotion to the Eucharist—has a lot to do with "fully appropriating and internalizing what each of us has acknowledged as *our life*, with all its unique sorrows and joys" (BJ:May 12). It surely pays to subject our life to examination time and again so we can maximize our way of spending it. As Lillian Dickson put it, "Life is like a coin; you can spend it any way you wish, but you only spend it once."[6]

People who possess a profound sense of their value enjoy life to the fullest—"precisely because they are in touch with the life-giving quality of their existence. Their joy brings forth joy, and their peace brings forth peace. They make us aware of the holy contagiousness of all that lives" (LS:56). We have every reason indeed to celebrate the vitality of life.

Henri Nouwen uncovers the deep secret behind every authentic celebration of life:

The life we celebrate is not imprisoned within the boundaries of birth and death; it is not caught in the fatalism of chronology; it is not based on the little bits of happiness with which our world tempts us, such as success, popularity or power. No, the life we celebrate is...the life of God given to us from all eternity to all eternity.[7]

"God is a God of life" and "[a] life with God opens us to all that is alive." God enjoins us to "celebrate life," making us "desire to always be where life is" (LC:75).

We have always belonged and will always belong to God. The eternal truth of our identity is that we are the beloved of God before our birth, and we remain the beloved even after our death. "Life," Nouwen points out, "is just an interruption of eternity, just a little opportunity for a few years to say, 'I love you, too.'"[8] As we celebrate life, we are, in a special way, responding in love with our hearts fully alive to the God of life and love. Needless to say, our precious time on earth is relatively short and we want to seize every opportunity to savor each significant celebration of life we encounter.

Indeed, "our short lives on earth are sowing times" and "this wonderful knowledge that nothing we live in our bodies is lived in vain holds a call for us to live every moment as a seed for eternity" (*BJ*:Nov 29). Life is an investment. People can benefit through our life as we go on bearing fruit even after we die since "the legacy we leave for the people we have known finds its fullness after we are gone."[9]

Befriending Death

As we learn to meaningfully celebrate and befriend life, we should be able to do the same when it comes to the whole notion of death. Doing so does not mean we have to romanticize death, because it will continue to remain our enemy, so to speak, something for which we will never find ourselves totally prepared. Just the same, it may be worth thinking through the following set of questions that Henri Nouwen poses:

> Is death such an absolute end of all our thoughts and actions that we simply cannot face it? Or is it possible to befriend our dying gradually and live open to it, trusting that we have nothing to fear? Is it possible to prepare for death with the same attentiveness that our parents had in preparing for our birth? Can we wait for our death as for a friend who wants to welcome us home? (*GG*:xiii)

In answer to his own questions, Nouwen is convinced that his suggestions are not only possible but critically necessary. Repeating himself, he urges us: "We have to prepare ourselves for our death with the same care and attention as our parents prepared themselves for our birth" (*BJ*:Dec 3).

In fact, it makes absolute sense "that we face death before we are in any real danger of dying and reflect on our mortality before all our conscious and unconscious energy is directed to the struggle to survive" (*LC*:28). Henri Nouwen convincingly argued that if only we could engage death as a familiar guest as opposed to an intimidating stranger, "we would be able to shed many of our doubts and insecurities, face our mortality, and live as free people."[10] With this reframing of our perspective, death need not be an unwanted or utterly dreaded enemy, but rather a potential friend that we can bravely welcome.

How exactly can we befriend death then? Before answering this question, let me first direct our focus to what Henri Nouwen firmly establishes as the necessary foundation for this task: "the power of love [which] is stronger than the power of death" itself (*LC*:34). The potency of real, deep, human love—one that "will always reach out toward the eternal" and "is not willing to be imprisoned by time"—is what exposes the utter absurdity of death and is the very thing that can enable us to befriend it (*LC*:32–33). True love, as the trite expression goes, is indeed forever. To be more specific, it is this quality of human love flowing out of the reality of divine love that overcomes both life and death.

Befriending death requires that we claim both the essence of our being beloved of God as well as our inherent freedom as his children, according to Henri Nouwen. Doing so strips death of its power over us, "liberate[s] our death from its absurdity and make[s] it the gateway to a new life" (*GG*:18, 47). When we embrace Jesus' way of living and dying, "we can face death with the mocking question of the apostle Paul: 'Death, where is your victory? Death, where is your sting?' [1 Corinthians 15:55]" (*GG*:47).

When we deliberately try to befriend this enemy called death, our often-morbid perspective toward it vanishes slowly. We begin to see it in a new and much different light. Death can appropriately be construed as "a passage to new life" (*BJ*:Aug 22). The hidden gift of dying is the fact that "we will make our passage to new life in solidarity with all the people of the earth" (*GG*:26). Henri Nouwen expounds on what he believes is the uniting power of death:

But if we grow in awareness that our mortality, more than anything else, will lead us into solidarity with others, then death can become a celebration of our unity with the human race. Instead of separating us from others, death can unite us with others; instead of being sorrowful, it can give rise to new joy; instead of simply ending life, it can begin something new. (*GG*:27)

Just as a well-lived life can bring forth fruit from which others benefit, so can our death. Thus, "dying well means dying for others, making our lives fruitful for those we leave behind" (*BJ*:Feb 10). So the real question that Henri Nouwen poses as you and I consider our own death is not: "How much can I still accomplish before I die, or how many things can I still do?" The real question is: "How can I prepare myself for my death in such a way that my death can bear fruit for others?"[11] What are we bequeathing to the generation after ours? Our death must not only imprint a beautiful memory in people's minds but also effect a lasting impact that can change how people decide to live their lives differently.

Henri Nouwen's view that the task of befriending our death is also meant to serve others (*GG*:4) is based upon Christ's own life and death and resurrection. He explains:

We are challenged to look at him dying on the cross and to find there the meaning of our own life and death. What strikes me most…is that Jesus of Nazareth did not die for himself, but for us, and that in following him we too are called to make our death a death for others. (*LC*:58–59)

Nouwen was brought face to face with this realization in 1989, while he was in the process of recovery from surgery, during which he had a near brush with death. In one of his reflections published in *Beyond the Mirror*, he writes, "What I learned about dying is that I am called to die for others" and that, in a profound way, "dying is the most important act of living" (*BM*:63–64).

Henri Nouwen, therefore, concludes that "life is a long journey of preparation—of preparing oneself to truly die for others" (*BM*:65). In the process of it all, "we *can choose* to befriend our death as Jesus did. We *can choose* to live as God's beloved children in solidarity with all people, trusting in our ultimate fruit-fulness" (*GG*:48).

Embracing Both Life and Death

Michelle O'Rourke's beautiful book on a spirituality of dying highlights best for us what befriending both our life and death entails:

> Befriending our death comes through befriending our life. Henri's reflections gave birth to contemplating his own life and death, and can help us to do the same. Seeing ourselves as God's beloved, claiming that truth through prayer and reflection to let it shape the way we live, and understanding how our lives can become even more fruitful after we die, are important elements in befriending our inevitable death. Learning to live well not only enables us to embrace our dying, it helps us prepare ourselves to die well.[12]

Henri Nouwen is completely persuaded that "when we are ready to die at any moment, we are also ready to live at any moment" (*BJ*:Aug 27). Such an attitude refuses to isolate our perspective on life from our perspective on death, for they are existentially bound together. Moreover, "confronting our death ultimately allows us better to live. And better to dance with God's joy amid the sorrowing nights and the hopeful mornings," Nouwen affirms.[13]

Deep inside, we want to believe that life goes well beyond our mere experience of death—that everlasting life is not just a figment of our imagination. Yet Nouwen insists that "only by facing our mortality can we come in touch with the life that transcends death" (*BJ*:Feb 26). Death can and does crystallize the reality of the life eternal that is beyond life and death.

LIFE AND DEATH: FACING THE DILEMMA

The apostle Paul, in his letter to the believers in Philippi, poignantly expresses his own dilemma concerning the realities of life and death. He says: "For to me, living is Christ and dying is gain. If I am to live in the flesh, that means fruitful labor for me;

and I do not know which I prefer. I am hard pressed between the two: my desire is to depart and be with Christ, for that is far better; but to remain in the flesh is more necessary for you" (Phil 1:21–24).

Henri Nouwen comments that most of us are probably more inclined to grab onto our mortal life as much as we can. He wonders whether this tendency reveals that "we have lost contact with one of the most essential aspects of our creed: the faith in eternal life" (*BM*:78). Yet Nouwen also acknowledges that as we experience the deepening of our own communion with God, "we gradually get in touch with our desire to move through the gate of death into eternal life with Christ," much like the strong desire Paul himself expressed to the Philippians (*BJ*:Dec 2).

Nouwen paraphrases Paul's sentiments as follows: "I want to be gone and to be with Christ, and this is by far the stronger desire—and yet for your sake to stay alive in this body is a more urgent need" (*HN*:141). We can see how, in his own unique way, Paul learned to befriend both life and death for different reasons. He found no trouble continuing to live his new life in Christ the way he always had, maximizing it for the sake of the people to whom he was seeking to minister. Yet at the same time, he was also eager to taste death in order that he might finally go home to be with Christ in glory.

In both cases, one thing stands out as obvious: whether it be life or death, Christ served as the motivating force for Paul. In a way, the tension brought on by the dilemma he was confronting seemed to dissolve in the face of Christ, the Christ who was his very reason for living and dying. As believers, the ultimate matters of life and death, along with their inherent tension, take on an entirely different meaning when we are able to articulate clearly what we are willing to live and/or die for. As long as Christ stays elevated at the center of our experience of life and death, our alleged dilemma can gradually devolve into a nonissue altogether.

Christ is the ultimate reason to celebrate both life and death. We can, after all, affirm with a resounding Amen that climactic declaration with which Paul himself solidly assures each one of us: that "neither death, nor life...will be able to separate us from the love of God in Christ Jesus our Lord" (Rom 8:38–39).

We have just unpacked the trilogy of tensions—inward, outward, and upward—along with the psychological, ministerial, and theological dynamics sparked by the various sets of spiritual polarities we have discussed. In the process, we caught glimpses of how Henri Nouwen learned to live with their realities in a way that supported the holistic thrust of his journey. By way of concluding, we can ask ourselves this summary question: How can we do the same as we squarely face our own tension-laden existence?

❧

Life/Death

FOR PERSONAL REFLECTION

1. Based on how I live, what does that reveal about my current views on life and death? What would it entail for me "to live in order to die"?

2. How does my celebrating life become a concrete and meaningful response to the God of life and love?

3. Am I willing to embrace both life and death with equal passion? How do I navigate my way through this tension and squarely face this seeming dilemma?

Suggested Reflective Exercise

CRADLE AND GRAVE

When was the last time you glimpsed a newborn baby or attended to a dying person? What immediately comes to mind when you entertain the sight of a "cradle" and a "grave" simultaneously?

Muse over these questions for a while; hold and contain them in the silence of your heart. Sort through your emotions and feelings and seek to discover a creative outlet for them.

How would you represent them through a collection of pictures, a collage, or a simple sketch? Respond to however you are being led in the moment.

Visualize what it might look like for you to celebrate both life and death with total abandon. End this exercise in gratitude to God for the mystery of life and death!

CONCLUSION

Befriending Tension

In analyzing Henri Nouwen's unique way of construing reality, Phil Zylla, professor of pastoral theology at McMaster Divinity College in Hamilton, Ontario, suggests that Nouwen must have possessed what he calls a "paradigmatic" mind—a "way of viewing" as well as "sense-making" that incorporates a highly shaded and sophisticated level of conceptualization. In an essay he wrote on this topic—which was based on a presentation he gave during the first international conference held in Toronto coinciding with the tenth anniversary of Henri Nouwen's death—Zylla highlights the paradigmatic contours of Nouwen's thinking, which I can only attempt to condense here for the purpose of underlining Nouwen's integrative genius.[1]

Nouwen's conceptual framework, while rooted in his core ideas, always opens itself up to ever-increasing insight and more expansive reflection. His paradoxical language never fails to connect with lived reality. Comfortable and always prepared to hold mystery at its foundation, Nouwen's paradigmatic mind does not shun the challenge of living with the questions, while all the time being attentive to the intricacies and complexities of life itself.

Zylla's extensive application of the paradigmatic to Nouwen —the nuances of which I have barely touched on here—reinforces the notion of a certain framework of thinking and seeing that is sophisticated enough for one to feel at home with polarities and be able to deal with the tensions inherent in them. Henri Nouwen, without question, possessed a highly developed quality of mystical awareness—a keen combination of contemplative seeing and thinking that all of us are capable of cultivating as we move into a greater sense of wholeness and higher levels of integration.

Henri Nouwen saw things differently and operated out of a different framework of thinking because he personified the non-dualistic consciousness characteristic of the contemplative mystics. Ever mindful of how all of life is ultimately interconnected, Nouwen pursued all efforts at integration as a worthwhile investment and expenditure of his energy.

Most everyone knows that Henri Nouwen's life was itself a web of paradoxes, and that as a person, he embodied inner polarities and all manner of inconsistencies and contradictions—creative as well as painful ones. Close friends Bart and Patricia Gavigan commented that in Nouwen's life, "abundance and deprivation were side by side" and "celebration's brightness flowered on the edge of self-destructive darkness."[2] Like many of us, Henri Nouwen "taught best what he needed to learn most,"[3] and ironically, as most of his journal meditations demonstrate, "at his worst, Nouwen was at his best."[4]

One of Nouwen's friends during their student days in Holland describes Nouwen's personal conundrum:

> The most tragic yet most creative contradiction was implied in his inability to live out what he wrote. This was a source of great sadness for him and a reason for some to question the validity of his ideas and his credibility as a spiritual guide. The paradox is that he would never have become an inspirational spiritual writer if he had lived what he wrote. Therefore, his personal tragedy was also his gift to others.[5]

Biographer Michael Ford says the same thing in different words: "Angst was the signature tune of Nouwen, who brought hope and faith to millions through the struggles he dared to share."[6] Suffice it to say, Nouwen's gift of struggles—costly as it was for him—had an incredible healing effect upon others.

For Henri Nouwen, the personal tensions and contradictions of his life, just like many of our own contradictions, served as vehicles that "create the friction that can help us move toward God" because they "bring us in touch with a deeper longing for the fulfillment of a desire that lives beneath all desires and that only God can satisfy" (*BJ*:Apr 20). Such inner tensions, thus understood, can only be transformative.

Tension, regardless of how it might have expressed itself—whether inner or outer—became for Henri Nouwen like a close, intimate companion and friend on the journey. With the same open-heartedness that he greeted the reality of mystery in his life, Nouwen not only worked comfortably with spiritual polarities, but thrived in the accompanying tensions those polarities triggered within him. Like ours, his entire spiritual journey, as he came to accept it, was constantly characterized by a life of tension!

Befriending Tension

Tension. Just what do we do with it? Referencing Julian of Norwich's ability to hold tension, Thomas Merton wrote: "This is, for her, the heart of theology: not solving the contradiction, but remaining in the midst of it."[7] Since tension is an inevitable component of our existence and guaranteed to typify our journey experience, we might as well learn, like Julian, to remain in the midst of it. Better yet, we can follow Nouwen's example by learning to befriend the tensions arising from the spiritual polarities we encounter.

Nouwen encourages us to do just that. We can and should "become aware of the different poles between which our lives vacillate and are held in tension," precisely because such polarities "offer the context in which we can speak about the spiritual life" far more realistically (*RO*:18). Tension can be our friend—in fact, a gift and a blessing!

How then can we navigate our way through our tension-filled journey and allow it to work for us instead of against us? Drawing from Nouwen's life example, let me set forth three conditions through which we can embrace tension and reckon it as our friend as we press forward on our own journey.

Subscribing to a "Both/And" Modality

First, we need to cultivate the ability to nuance our oftentimes rigid perception of life and be willing to erase our illusion that everything can be classified as black or white, even if our waking experience continues to convince us otherwise. Henri Nouwen "was able to live with the gray"[8] because he knew on the intuitive level—as we should too—that life does not work on an "either/or" mode all the time. Still, our obsession with control fuels our stubborn insistence that it should.

Once we move away from this type of illusory notion and start acknowledging the possibility of another shade of reality, we can welcome the freeing potential of living in a "both/and" modality. As we do this, we might even begin to wonder how we could possibly have lived most of our life chained to such a constricting mindset as the "either/or" dichotomy. As Richard Rohr reveals, "A binary system of either/or choices is good and necessary in the lofty worlds of logic, mechanics, mathematics, and science," but when it comes to the realm of the spiritual, "it cannot access eternal things."[9]

Trying to live with an open mind that is willing to accommodate opposites—including moral ones—can relieve some of the tension that is aggravated when we gravitate toward polarity thinking. Here again, we see Henri Nouwen as "way ahead of his time in his implied critique of moral binary oppositions."[10] Developing and nurturing this kind of "both/and" mentality reinforces our capacity to learn "how to hold creative tensions, how to live with paradox and contradictions, how not to run from mystery."[11]

We have seen in numerous instances how Henri Nouwen refused to pit opposites against each other, but intentionally worked with them side by side in an effort to make far greater sense of reality than dualistic thinking is able to deliver. By creatively blurring, if not totally collapsing, their seemingly antithetical nature and placing them alongside each other, Nouwen was able to reach a more nuanced understanding of several opposite constructs. Such subtle nuancing, when applied to our specific context, often brings about deeper resonance to our spirit and consequently does justice to the complexity of our journey's reality. In the following reflection, Nouwen highlights how a dialectical framework of thinking broadens, instead of narrows, our overall perspective on life:

> It seems that there is not clear-cut joy, but that even in the most happy moments of our existence we sense a tinge of sadness. In every satisfaction, there is an awareness of its limitations. In every success there is fear of jealousy. Behind every smile, there is a tear. In every embrace, there is loneli-

ness. In every friendship, distance. And in all forms of light, there is the knowledge of surrounding darkness. (*OS*:xx)

It is obvious that an "either/or" mindset limits, while "both/and" expands our vision of reality. Our goal should be to capture a fuller sense of our lived reality as much as possible, and not to settle for a partial view and experience of it. Adopting such a "both/and" modality supports this positive direction.

Moving Closer to the Center

Another practical way to befriend tension is to make sure we are not constantly finding ourselves off center in terms of our view or position on things. "We are a circumference people, with little access to the center," Rohr avows.[12] Not only do we often locate our lives on the boundaries, but we easily fall into lopsidedness in our thinking. We tend to see narrowly or in a myopic fashion, utilizing only the selective lenses that make us comfortable. We refuse to entertain any other point of view even though we know that we are limited by our own. Author Madeleine L'Engle reminds us: "I have a point of view. You have a point of view. But *God* has *view*."[13] God does occupy the center point of everything—which is also the still point.

When it comes to the liberty of choosing sides on any matter, it is all too easy for us to let the pendulum swing to one extreme— either to the right or to the left—and conveniently bypass the middle. This carries over in the rigid attitudes we adopt concerning our political as well as religious views. We are only too swift to categorize our own position (as well as others') as either conservative or liberal. Henri Nouwen did not welcome such unwarranted labeling. He lamented:

> In religious circles, we often divide people into two camps: believers and nonbelievers, churched and unchurched, conservatives and progressives, orthodox and non-orthodox, saint and sinner. Characterization is common but narrowing. Labeling is always limiting. (*SF*:11)

Specifically, labeling people "left" or "right" has become a convenient rhetoric for classifying their positions. Employing either term somehow affords us the illusion that we have people all figured out—that we can actually "box" them and thereby deal with and manage their presence around us more easily. Henri Nouwen was hard to pin down as either to the right or to the left on the spectrum. As one interviewee for a film documentary on Nouwen's life commented, "You cannot call Henri liberal or conservative; he is radical."[14] His radicalism—without superficiality —makes it difficult, if not impossible, to pigeonhole Nouwen so easily.

Centrists are hard to come by because most find it knotty to assume the middle ground. Some even think that camping in the middle is tantamount to wallowing in compromise. We much prefer to stake out our position so as not to leave any room for others to speculate about where we are on any issue. Being definitive conveys decisiveness and feeds our inner need for some semblance of security and control. Henri Nouwen, in the latter part of his journey, admitted to reaching a point where he had to let crumble his own constructed "fences" and defenses that he had spent a lifetime building around people. Applying his newfound freedom in light of his reframed vision of community, Nouwen confessed,

> The great Christian call is not to be different but to be the same; not to wander off to the periphery of life where I might discover some small differences but to go to the center where I realize my solidarity with all human beings.[15]

When it comes to our adherence to certain truths or moral principles that govern our lives, there is a world of wisdom wrapped up in the saying that truth lies in the middle of two extremes. We may not always strike a good balance in our continuing pursuit of truth, but that is not a good excuse to allow ourselves to constantly fall to one side or the other. L'Engle assures us: "The center is always there, waiting for us to discover it."[16] For those willing and able to accommodate both the collision and coincidence of contraries, there is room for a "Third Way," the *tertium quid*—which Rohr likes to refer to as the real contemplative stance—that may well emerge for us.[17] In short, we need to be more intentional about moving as close as possible to the center and there be able to hold the tension better—that is, in a far less, if not totally nonpolarizing way. Deciding to go for the *via media* in the face of obvious contraries by no means eliminates tension; it does, however, cushion the brunt of it and conserves our energy, since we are no longer required to deal with extreme options and demands for closure or complete resolution.

Working toward Integration

The final suggestion I have for befriending tension is to exert a conscious effort to embrace a more integrative mindset. More often than not, we prefer splitting things off than welding them together. Instead of maintaining an exclusionary stance, we can choose to be more inclusive. One Yale graduate who shared a small-group experience with Henri Nouwen once remarked, "Henri's thought and approach stretch all the limits and boundaries, probably to the breaking point. His was and is a radical inclusivity that expands the faith beyond conventional limits."[18]

Integration promotes the task of inclusion and resists the pull toward exclusion. The capacity to integrate is really a mark of growth toward maturity—an increasing movement toward wholeness in our journey. Working toward integration relates to the elusive pursuit of balance—"the ability to control contrasting forces and bring them together in a creative way."[19]

The great Martin Luther King, Jr., who undeniably influenced Nouwen through his radical brand of contemplative action, once stated, "Life at its best is a creative synthesis of opposites in fruitful harmony."[20] Integrative thinking is a classic non-dual way of processing reality that does not dismiss, separate, subtract, or divide. It is the quality of thinking and seeing that "refuses to eliminate the negative, the problematic, the threatening parts of everything" but instead "receives it all."[21] To be sure, Henri Nouwen aligned himself with such a nonexclusive mindset, as Carolyn Whitney-Brown attests:

> To Henri, our human problems and struggles were to be transformed and used, not removed. Nothing needed to be rejected. Henri's understanding was deeply coherent with the whole philosophy undergirding L'Arche, with its refusal to accept simplistic dichotomies of good and bad, useful and useless, normal and handicapped.[22]

To use Richard Rohr's famous phrase, in God's economy, "everything belongs."[23] Henri Nouwen directs our attention to the fact that our heart "is the central unifying organ of our personal life" (*WOH*:77) wherein ultimate reality resides. As Jesus himself, in veiled reference to the mysterious notion of the Kingdom, implied: "For the Ultimate Reality is 'within you'!" (Luke 17:21).[24] Nouwen understood that reality, in the final analysis, is only in God for "nothing is real without deriving its reality from God" (*G*:49). "Reality *is* One," Rohr carefully emphasizes, and religion's task concerns "putting our divided realities back together."[25]

The call to solidarity with the entire human race, as Henri Nouwen clearly understood it, involves a willful movement from exclusion to inclusion marked by a more radical form of hospitality toward a larger, broader community, while openly embracing a greater sense of mystery (*SF*:90). Indeed, the real essence of inclusivity is "to live with the heart of God and together with all people."[26] For "it is in the heart of God...that we can come to the full realization of the unity of all that is." (*BJ*:Nov 16). Thus, Nouwen openly and boldly declares to one and all:

> There, in a[n]...experience of solidarity with the whole human race, we too, may witness many walls and boundaries come tumbling down...[O]n a deeper level, we can realize our common humanity. In the light of God's unconditional love and our own belovedness, we may experience our hearts expanding as if there are no limits. In the community of the heart, no one is excluded. (*SF*:94)

Love is what ultimately brings everything together in perfect unity and harmony: "the heart of God, the heart of all creation, and our own hearts" (*BJ*:Nov 16). The essence of integration is our conscious movement and growth toward greater love, unity, inclusion, wholeness, and harmony.

In summary, we cannot afford not to learn how to befriend the glaring existence of tension in our journey. It is what it is, no matter what. We are the ones who need to adjust. Therefore, every effort we invest counts—including subscribing to a "both/and" modality, moving closer to the center, and working toward integration—toward mastering the art of living with tension by gradually seeing everything differently, using a new set of eyes. Richard Rohr sums up this all-important truth for us: "We do not see things as they are; we see things as we are."[27] Henri Nouwen definitely saw things as he was!

Notes

Preface

1. Wil Hernandez, *Henri Nouwen: A Spirituality of Imperfection* (Mahwah, NJ: Paulist, 2006).

2. Wil Hernandez, *Henri Nouwen and Soul Care: A Ministry of Integration* (Mahwah, NJ: Paulist, 2008).

3. Richard Rohr, *The Naked Now: Learning to See as the Mystics See* (New York: Crossroad, 2009).

4. See Richard Rohr, *Falling Upward: A Spirituality for the Two Halves of Life* (San Francisco: Jossey-Bass, 2011), 146–151.

5. Carolyn Whitney-Brown, "How Not to Comfort a New Orleans Hurricane Survivor," in *Turning the Wheel: Henri Nouwen and Our Search for God*, ed. Jonathan Bengtson and Gabrielle Earnshaw (Maryknoll, NY: Orbis, 2007), 143–144.

6. Rohr, *Naked Now*, 122.

7. Ibid., 123.

8. Don McNeill, interview by Karen Pascal, in *Journey of the Heart: The Life of Henri Nouwen* (Markham, ON: Windborne Productions, 2001).

Introduction

1. Rohr, *Naked Now*, 105 (see preface, n. 3).

2. Jeremy Wiebe, "Otherness and Justice in the Thought of Paul Ricoeur and Henri Nouwen," in *Turning the Wheel*, 81 (see preface, n. 5).

3. Robert K. Johnston, *Useless Beauty: Ecclesiastes through the Lens of Contemporary Film* (Grand Rapids, MI: Baker, 2004), 33.

4. Cf. J. I. Packer, *Evangelism and the Sovereignty of God* (Downers Grove, IL: InterVarsity, 1961), 18–21.

5. Rohr, *Naked Now*, 98–99.

6. Preston Busch, "Unresolved Tensions? The Life and Thought

of Henri Nouwen from 1932–1981" (MDiv thesis, Briarcrest Biblical Seminary, 2001), viii–ix.

7. Ibid., 6.

8. Robert A. Jonas, ed., *Henri Nouwen: Writings Selected with an Introduction by Robert A. Jonas* (Maryknoll, NY: Orbis, 1998), xxxv.

9. Busch, "Unresolved Tensions?" 6.

10. Hernandez, *Henri Nouwen: A Spirituality of Imperfection*, 75 (see preface, n. 1).

Part I: Living with *Inward* Polarities

CHAPTER ONE: TRUE SELF AND FALSE SELF

1. Mary Jo Leddy, "We Are Weak and Strong as God Is Merciful and Just," in *Turning the Wheel*, 4 (see preface, n. 5).

2. See *Breakthrough: Meister Eckhart's Creation Spirituality in New Translation*, introduction and commentary by Matthew Fox (Garden City, NY: Image, 1980), 118.

3. Thomas Merton, *New Seeds of Contemplation* (New York: New Directions, 1961), 34.

4. Henri Nouwen, "Contemplation and Action," sermon preached at St. Paul's Church, Columbia University, December 10, 1978 (The Henri J. M. Nouwen Archives and Research Collection, John M. Kelly Library, University of St. Michael's College, Toronto), 3.

5. I owe this wonderful description from my secondary mentor at Fuller Seminary, Dr. David Augsburger.

6. John S. Mogabgab, "When You See, You See Direct! Turning the Wheel to Sharpen your Sight," in *Turning the Wheel*, 221.

7. M. Basil Pennington, *True Self, False Self: Unmasking the Spirit Within* (New York: Crossroad, 2000), 46.

8. Henri Nouwen, *Beloved: Henri Nouwen in Conversation with Philip Roderick* (Toronto: Novalis, 2007), 13.

9. See M. Robert Mulholland, Jr., *The Deeper Journey: The Spirituality of Discovering Your True Self* (Downers Grove, IL: InterVarsity, 2006), 30. See also Albert Haase, OFM, *Coming Home to Your True Self: Leaving the Emptiness of False Attractions* (Downers Grove, IL: InterVarsity, 2008), 50–51.

10. I am not here deliberately addressing the right biblical solution to the problem of the false self as that is beyond the scope and thrust of this particular chapter. Nouwen himself did not deal directly with the dilemma portrayed by Paul in Romans 7. The pri-

mary focus here is on how Nouwen handled the tension brought on by the coexistence of the true self and the false self and not on offering the answer to the dilemma per se. For an excellent scriptural treatment of this specific issue, see chapter 4 of Mulholland, *The Deeper Journey*, 68–98.

11. Merton, *New Seeds of Contemplation*, 34.

12. Pennington, *True Self, False Self*, 31.

13. Sue Monk Kidd, *When the Heart Waits: Spiritual Direction for Life's Sacred Questions* (San Francisco: HarperSanFrancisco, 1990), 58.

14. Ibid., 73.

15. Whitney-Brown, "How Not to Comfort a New Orleans Hurricane Survivor," in *Turning the Wheel*, 136.

16. See Eugene H. Peterson, *Under the Unpredictable Plant: An Exploration in Vocational Holiness* (Grand Rapids, MI: Eerdmans, 1992), 6.

17. Quoted in Michael Ford, *Spiritual Masters for All Seasons* (Mahwah, NJ: Hidden Spring, 2009), 71.

18. Kidd, *When the Heart Waits*, 49–50.

CHAPTER TWO: SELF-OWNING AND SELF-GIVING

1. See a more thorough discussion of this theme in my first book, *Henri Nouwen: A Spirituality of Imperfection*, 23ff. (see preface, n. 1).

2. Stephen Kendrick, "In Touch with the Blessing: An Interview with Henri Nouwen," *Christian Century* (March 1993): 319.

3. James R. Newby and Elizabeth Newby, *Between Peril and Promise* (Nashville: Thomas Nelson, 1984), 40.

4. See Peter Brown, *The Body and Society: Men, Women, and Sexual Renunciation in Early Christianity* (New York: Columbia University Press, 1988), 229.

5. Henri Nouwen and Walter J. Gafney, *Aging: The Fulfillment of Life* (New York: Image, 1990), 117.

6. Nouwen, *Journey of the Heart* video (see preface, n. 8).

7. See Henri Nouwen, "Living in the Center Enables Us to Care," *Health Progress* 71 (July/August 1990): 53.

8. Cf. Thomas Merton, *Thoughts on Solitude* (Boston: Shambhala, 1993), 3, 20.

9. David G. Benner, *The Gift of Being Yourself: The Sacred Call to Self-Discovery* (Downers Grove: InterVarsity, 2004), 17.

10. Ibid., 97, 101.

11. Hernandez, *Henri Nouwen and Soul Care*, 55 (see preface, n. 2).

CHAPTER THREE: WOUNDEDNESS AND HEALING

1. Benner, *The Gift of Being Yourself*, 53 (see chap. 2, no 9). As Richard Rohr explains it, "we tend to overidentify with one part of ourselves. We reject our weaknesses and we overwork our strengths" (*Everything Belongs: The Gift of Contemplative Prayer* [New York: Crossroad, 1999], 137).

2. Benner, *The Gift of Being Yourself*, 54.

3. Ray S. Anderson, *On Being Human: Essays in Theological Anthropology* (Pasadena, CA: Fuller Seminary Press, 1982), 214.

4. Henri Nouwen, *Turn My Mourning into Dancing: Finding Hope in Hard Times*, compiled and edited by Timothy Jones (Nashville: Word, 2001), 12.

5. Wayne Muller, *A Life of Being, Having, and Doing Enough* (New York: Three Rivers, 2010), 145.

6. From Jean Vanier's eulogy during Nouwen's funeral in Holland as quoted by Sue Mosteller in Nouwen, *Sabbatical Journey: The Diary of His Final Year* (New York: Crossroad, 2000), ix.

7. Quoted in Philip Simmons, *Learning to Fall: The Blessings of an Imperfect Life* (New York: Bantam, 2002), 32.

8. Rohr, *Everything Belongs*, 141. Rohr further comments that even Julian of Norwich viewed God as reckoning our wounds as "honors" or "trophies" or, as one other Julian scholar renders it, our wounds are "'awards' in the sense that the wounds are made 'badges of grace'" (see Fr. John-Julian, OJN, *The Complete Julian of Norwich* [Brewster, MA: Paraclete, 2009], 184).

9. See Hernandez, *Henri Nouwen: A Spirituality of Imperfection*, 76 (see preface, n. 1). Cf. Frederick Buechner, *The Longing for Home: Recollections and Reflections* (New York: HarperCollins, 1996), 109–110.

10. Rev. Gregory Jensen, "The Work of Henri Nouwen as a Meeting Place for Eastern and Western Christians," in *Turning the Wheel*, 11 (see preface, n. 5).

11. Ibid.

Part II: Living with *Outward* Polarities

CHAPTER FOUR: SOLITUDE AND COMMUNITY

1. Michael Ford, *Wounded Prophet: A Portrait of Henri J. M. Nouwen* (New York: Doubleday, 1999), 5–6.

2. Dietrich Bonhoeffer, *Life Together: A Discussion of Christian Fellowship* (San Francisco: HarperSanFrancisco, 1954), 77–78.

3. See Henri Nouwen, "Moving from Solitude to Community to Ministry," *Leadership* (Spring 1995): 81, and *Spiritual Direction: Wisdom for the Long Walk of Faith,* ed. Michael J. Christensen and Rebecca J. Laird (New York: HarperCollins, 2006), 110. I already addressed this theme thoroughly in my second book (see *Henri Nouwen and Soul Care*, 56–60 [see preface, n. 2]) so I am simply highlighting it here.

4. See Hernandez, *Henri Nouwen: A Spirituality of Imperfection*, 33–38 (see preface, n. 1).

5. Arthur Boers, "What Henri Nouwen Found at Daybreak: Experiments in Spiritual Living in a Secular World," *Christianity Today* 38 (October 3, 1994): 28.

6. The integration or "coinherence" of spirituality and ministry is itself addressed quite extensively in chapter two of my first book (see *Henri Nouwen: A Spirituality of Imperfection*, 26–53 [see preface, n. 1]).

7. Henri Nouwen, "Contemplation and Ministry," *Sojourners* 7 (June 1978): 11.

8. Ibid.

9. Parker J. Palmer, *The Active Life: Wisdom for Work, Creativity, and Caring* (San Francisco: HarperSanFrancisco, 1990), 15. Parker's proposal is a good example of what philosopher Gaston Bachelard refers to as an artificial syntax—in which the outside features of the word blend with the inside by multiplication of hyphens (see *The Poetics of Space* [Boston: Beacon, 1969], 213).

10. Phileena Heurtz, "Contemplative Activism: A Transformative Way," *Conversations: A Forum for Authentic Transformation* 8.2 (Fall/Winter 2010): 47.

11. Henri J. M. Nouwen, "Compassion: The Core of Spiritual Leadership," *Occasional Papers, The Institute for Ecumenical and Cultural Research* 2 (March 1977): 1–6.

12. Cited in Philip Sheldrake, *Spaces for the Sacred: Place, Memory and Identity* (London: SCM, 2002), 128.

13. Ibid., 140.

14. Henri J. M. Nouwen, "Intimacy, Fecundity, and Ecstasy," *Radix* (May/June 1984): 10.

15. Three of Nouwen's books, in particular, *The Genesee Diary*, *A Cry for Mercy: Prayers from the Genessee* (New York: Image, 2002), and *Thomas Merton: Contemplative Critic* (Liguori, MO: Liguori/Triumph, 1991), all address "the integration of silent contemplation and social responsibility" (Jonas, ed., *Henri Nouwen*, xxxv [see introduction, n. 8]). See also John Dear, ed., *Road to Peace* (Maryknoll, NY: Orbis, 1998). Cf. Jurgen Beumer, *Henri Nouwen: A Restless Seeking God* (New York: Crossroad, 1997), 121–131.

16. Robert A. Jonas, ed., *The Essential Henri Nouwen* (Boston: Shambala, 2009), xxxi.

17. Philip Sheldrake, "Christian Spirituality as a Way of Living Publicly: A Dialectic of the Mystical and the Prophetic," *Spiritus: A Journal of Christian Spirituality* 3 (Spring 2003): 19.

CHAPTER FIVE: COMPASSION AND CONFRONTATION

1. See, for example, Nouwen's own public confession in his foreword to *We Drink from Our Own Wells: The Spiritual Journey of a People*, by Gustavo Gutiérrez (Maryknoll, NY: Orbis, 1984), xvi.

2. Thomas Merton, *Contemplation in a World of Action* (Garden City: Image, 1971), 154–155.

3. The ministry of soul care and companioning is the primary focus of my second book, *Henri Nouwen and Soul Care* (see preface, n. 2).

4. This was a catchy word coined by David Augsburger in his book *Caring Enough to Confront* (Scottdale, PA/Waterloo, ON: Herald, 1980), 11.

5. Ibid., 10.

6. Ibid.

7. I deal with this subject matter more extensively in my second book, *Henri Nouwen and Soul Care* (see preface, n. 2) (see particularly chapter one, 7ff.).

8. Jay M. Uomoto, "Human Suffering, Psychotherapy and Soul Care: The Spirituality of Henri Nouwen at the Nexus," *Journal of Psychology and Christianity* 14 (Winter 1995): 347, 352.

9. See the climax portion of the video *Journey of the Heart* (see preface, n. 8).

10. See for instance several wonderful accounts contained in Beth Porter with Susan M. S. Brown and Philip Coulter, eds., *Befriending Life: Encounters with Henri Nouwen* (New York:

Doubleday, 2001). Michael O'Laughlin, Nouwen's former teaching assistant at Harvard, points to Nouwen's caring attitude toward people as "perhaps his greatest attribute and his greatest teaching" ("Henri the Teacher," in *Remembering Henri,* ed. Gerald S. Twomey and Claude Pomerleau [Maryknoll, NY: Orbis, 2006], 7).

11. Siobhan Keogh, interview with the author, August 27, 2007.

12. Nathan Ball, "A Covenant of Friendship," in *Befriending Life,* 94.

13. Ibid., 97.

14. Sue Mosteller, interview with the author, April 26, 2004.

15. Cf. Henri Nouwen, "Education to Ministry," *Theological Education* 9 (Autumn 1972): 50.

16. Jean Vanier, "A Gentle Instrument of a Loving God," in *Befriending Life,* 261.

17. Nouwen's nephew, Marc van Campen, commented: "Henri did not push religion on me...but I did get some idea of what it meant for him...He made me see that it was a way of life, not distinct from our ordinary lives" ("Uncle Henri," in *Befriending Life,* 178–179).

18. See Hernandez, *Henri Nouwen and Soul Care.*

19. Deirdre LaNoue, *The Spiritual Legacy of Henri Nouwen* (New York: Continuum, 2000), 138.

20. Henri Nouwen, *The Only Necessary Thing: Living a Prayerful Life,* comp. and ed. Wendy Wilson Greer (New York: Crossroad, 1991), 19. Italics mine.

21. Or as Nouwen expressed in dismay, "One of the greatest problems of education remains that solutions are offered without the existence of a question," *Reaching Out: The Three Movements of the Spiritual Life* (New York: Image, 1975), 85.

22. Lisa Cataldo, "The Reality Principle," in *Befriending Life,* 62–63.

23. Peter Naus, "A Man of Creative Contradictions," in *Befriending Life,* 87.

CHAPTER SIX: PRESENCE AND ABSENCE

1. James D. Whitehead and Evelyn Eaton Whitehead, *Holy Eros: Pathways to a Passionate God* (Maryknoll, NY: Orbis, 2009), 149–150.

2. Ibid., 147.

3. O'Laughlin, "Henri the Teacher," in *Remembering Henri,* 4 (see chap. 5, n. 10).

4. Chris Glaser, "Henri's Greatest Gift," in *Befriending Life*, 133 (see chap. 5, n. 10).

5. See for instance, Wendy Lywood, "Rediscovering My Priesthood," in *Befriending Life*, 234.

6. This is a recasting of the summary I did for my first book based on the work of Jose Pananchimootil, "Heart Centered Spirituality for Ministers: The Life and Writings of Henri J. M. Nouwen" (Pars dissertationis ad lauream in Facultae S. Theologae apud Pontificiam Universitatem S. Thomae in Urbe, Romae: [s.n.], 2000), 87. Cf. Hernandez, *Henri Nouwen: A Spirituality of Imperfection*, 71 (see preface, n. 1).

7. David G. Benner, *Sacred Companions: The Gift of Spiritual Friendship and Direction* (Downers Grove, IL: InterVarsity, 2003), 51.

8. David G. Benner, *Soulful Spirituality: Becoming Fully Alive and Deeply Human* (Grand Rapids, MI: Brazos, 2011), 104.

Part III: Living with *Upward* Polarities

CHAPTER SEVEN: SUFFERING AND GLORY

1. Jürgen Moltmann, *Theology of Hope* (New York: Harper & Row, 1975), 16.

2. This and the two paragraphs that follow are reinstatements of the points I have already addressed in chapter five of my first book under the heading "Nature of Struggle" (*Henri Nouwen: A Spirituality of Imperfection*, 119–120 [see preface, n. 1]). It bears repeating them here as they clearly reinforce the arguments I am making in this particular section.

3. C. E. B. Cranfield, *The Epistle to the Romans*, The International Critical Commentary, ed. J. A. Emerton and C. E. B. Cranfield, vol. 1 (Edinburgh: T. & T. Clark, 1975), 356.

4. Nouwen, *Turn My Mourning into Dancing*, 9 (see chap. 3, n. 4).

5. C. S. Lewis, *A Mind Awake: An Anthology of C. S. Lewis*, ed. Clyde S. Kilby (New York: Harcourt, Brace & World, 1968), 21.

6. Nouwen, *Turn My Mourning into Dancing*, 79.

CHAPTER EIGHT: PRESENT AND FUTURE

1. As Larry J. Kreitzer puts it, "There exists in Paul a dialectic between the present and the future. The present is conditioned by both the past [death and resurrection of Jesus Christ] and the future [the awaited parousia at the end of time]" ("Eschatology," in

Dictionary of Paul and His Letters, ed. Gerald F. Hawthorne, Ralph P. Martin, and Daniel G. Reid [Downers Grove, IL: InterVarsity, 1993], 257).

2. David Wenham, "The Christian Life: A Life of Tension?" in *Pauline Studies*, ed. Donald A. Hagner and Murray J. Harris (Grand Rapids, MI: Eerdmans, 1980), 90.

3. Ibid., n. 94.

4. Gordon D. Fee, *Paul, the Spirit, and the People of God* (Peabody, MA: Hendrickson, 1996), 49.

5. George Eldon Ladd, *A Theology of the New Testament*, rev. ed., ed. Donald A. Hagner and Murray J. Harris (Grand Rapids, MI: Eerdmans, 1993, 1996), 568.

6. David Peterson, *Possessed by God* (Grand Rapids, MI: Eerdmans, 1995), 99.

7. This is a recasting of humorist Barbara Johnson's most quoted statement: "We are an Easter people living in a Good Friday world" (see *The Best Devotions of Barbara Johnson* [Grand Rapids, MI: Zondervan, 2001], 171).

8. James D. G. Dunn, *The Theology of Paul the Apostle* (Grand Rapids, MI: Eerdmans, 1998), 465.

9. David S. Dockery, "An Outline of Paul's View of the Spiritual Life: Foundations for an Evangelical Spirituality," in *Exploring Christian Spirituality: An Ecumenical Reader*, ed. Kenneth J. Collins (Grand Rapids, MI: Baker, 2000), 346–347.

10. Cranfield, *The Epistle to the Romans*, 369 (see chap. 7, n. 3).

11. Nouwen, *Turn My Mourning into Dancing*, 62 (see chap. 3, n. 4).

12. Phil Zylla, "Contours of the Paradigmatic in Henri Nouwen's Pastoral Theology," in *Turning the Wheel*, 209 (see preface, n. 5).

13. Rebecca Manley Pippert, *Hope Has Its Reasons* (San Francisco: Harper & Row, 1989), 204.

CHAPTER NINE: LIFE AND DEATH

1. Joseph Cardinal Bernardin, *The Gift of Peace* (Chicago: Loyola Press, 1997), 128.

2. Jonas, ed., *The Essential Henri Nouwen*, xliv (see chap. 4, n. 16).

3. Ibid., 50.

4. Nouwen, *Turn My Mourning into Dancing*, 96 (see chap. 3, n. 4).

5. Henri Nouwen, *Creative Ministry*, 94–95, as quoted in Jonas, ed., *The Essential Henri Nouwen*, 63 (edited for gender inclusivity).

6. Lillian Dickson (n.d.). FinestQuotes.com. Retrieved January 4, 2011, from http://www.finestquotes.com/author_quotes-author-Lillian Dickson-page-0.htm.

7. Henri Nouwen, "A Time to Mourn, A Time to Dance," 1992, Manuscript Series, Henri J. M. Nouwen Archives and Research Collection, John M. Kelly Library, University of St. Michael's College, Toronto, 8 (as cited in Michelle O'Rourke, *Befriending Death: Henri Nouwen and a Spirituality of Dying* [Maryknoll, NY: Orbis, 2009], 82).

8. Henri Nouwen, "Befriending Death" (transcript of a presentation at the National Catholic AIDS Network, Chicago, July 1995), Henri J. M. Nouwen Archives and Research Collection, John M. Kelly Library, University of St. Michael's College, Toronto, 5 (cited in O'Rourke, *Befriending Death*, 47).

9. O'Rourke, *Befriending Death*, 60.

10. Ibid., 43.

11. Henri Nouwen, "Henri Nouwen on Death and Aging," *Cross Point* (Fall 1995): 2.

12. O'Rourke, *Befriending Death*, 64.

13. Nouwen, *Turn My Mourning into Dancing*, 110.

Conclusion: Befriending Tension

1. To read the entire essay, see Zylla, "Contours of the Paradigmatic," in *Turning the Wheel*, 205–18 (see chap. 8, n. 12).

2. Bart and Patricia Gavigan, "Collision and Paradox," in *Befriending Life*, 55 (see chap. 5, n. 10).

3. Ibid., 56–57.

4. Ford, *Spiritual Masters for All Seasons*, 82 (see chap. 1, n. 17).

5. Naus, "A Man of Creative Contradictions," in *Befriending Life*, 84–85.

6. Ford, *Spiritual Masters for All Seasons*, 90.

7. Thomas Merton, *Conjectures of a Guilty Bystander* (Garden City, NY: Doubleday, 1996), 192.

8. See Mary Bastedo, "Henri and Daybreak: A Story of Mutual Transformation," in *Befriending Life*, 33.

9. Rohr, *Naked Now*, 106 (see preface, n. 3).

10. Whitney-Brown, "How Not to Comfort a New Orleans Hurricane Survivor," in *Turning the Wheel*, 142 (see preface, n. 5).

11. Ibid., 32.

12. Rohr, *Everything Belongs*, 15 (see chap. 3, n. 1).

13. Madeleine L'Engle, *Walking on Water: Reflections on Faith and Art* (Colorado Springs: Water Brook, 1980), 179.

14. McNeill, cited in video interview, *Journey of the Heart* (see preface, n. 8).

15. Henri Nouwen, "Spirituality of the Family," *Weavings* 3.1 (January/February 1988): 8.

16. L'Engle, *Walking on Water*, 227.

17. Rohr, *Everything Belongs*, 23.

18. Phillip N. Grigsby, "Aspects of Henri Nouwen's Social Ministry," in *Turning the Wheel*, 200.

19. Henri J. M. Nouwen, "Sermon: On Balance," in *Sermons and Meditations* (Yale Divinity School), University of St. Michael's College, John M. Kelly Library, Special Collections and Archives, Henri Nouwen Fonds, Box 36, 143.

20. Martin Luther King, Jr., *Strength to Love* (Philadelphia: Fortress, 1963), 13.

21. Rohr, *Naked Now*, 191.

22. Whitney-Brown, "How Not to Comfort a New Orleans Hurricane Survivor," in *Turning the Wheel*, 143.

23. See Rohr, *Everything Belongs*.

24. Rohr, *Naked Now*, 76.

25. Rohr, *Everything Belongs*, 116.

26. Grigsby, "Aspects of Henri Nouwen's Social Ministry," in *Turning the Wheel*, 201.

27. Ibid., 82.

Selected Bibliography

Primary Sources by Henri J. M. Nouwen

A Letter of Consolation. San Francisco: HarperSanFrancisco, 1982.

Beyond the Mirror: Reflections on Death and Life. New York: Crossroad, 2001.

Bread for the Journey: A Daybook of Wisdom and Faith. San Francisco: HarperSanFrancisco, 1997.

Can You Drink the Cup? Notre Dame: Ave Maria, 1996.

Clowning in Rome: Reflections on Solitude, Celibacy, Prayer, and Contemplation. New York: Image, 2000.

Compassion: A Reflection on the Christian Life. New York: Image, 1983.

Creative Ministry. New York: Image, 1978.

¡Gracias! A Latin American Journal. Maryknoll, NY: Orbis, 1993.

Here and Now: Living in the Spirit. New York: Crossroad, 1994.

In Memoriam. Notre Dame: Ave Maria Press, 1980.

In the Name of Jesus: Reflections on Christian Leadership. New York: Crossroad, 1989.

Letters to Marc about Jesus: Living a Spiritual Life in a Material World. San Francisco: HarperSanFrancisco, 1998.

Life of the Beloved: Spiritual Living in a Secular World. New York: Crossroad, 1992.

Lifesigns: Intimacy, Fecundity, and Ecstasy in Christian Perspective. New York: Doubleday, 1986.

Our Greatest Gift: A Meditation on Death and Dying. New York: HarperCollins, 1995.

Out of Solitude: Three Meditations on the Christian Life. Notre Dame: Ave Maria Press, 1974.

Reaching Out: The Three Movements of the Spiritual Life. New York: Doubleday, 1975.

Spiritual Direction: Wisdom for the Long Walk of Faith. New York: HarperOne, 2006.

Spiritual Formation: Following the Movements of the Spirit. New York: HarperOne, 2010.

The Genesee Diary: Report from a Trappist Monastery. New York: Image, 1989.

The Inner Voice of Love: A Journey Through Anguish to Freedom. New York: Image, 1996.

The Living Reminder: Service and Prayer in Memory of Jesus Christ. San Franciso: HarperSanFrancisco, 1977.

The Return of the Prodigal Son: A Story of Homecoming. New York: Image, 1994.

The Way of the Heart: Desert Spirituality and Contemporary Ministry. New York: HarperCollins, 1991.

The Wounded Healer: Ministry in Contemporary Society. New York: Image, 1979.

Walk with Jesus: Stations of the Cross. Maryknoll, NY: Orbis, 1990.

With Open Hands: Bringing Prayer into Your Life. New York: Ballantine, 1985.

Index

Special Thanks

to my faithful spiritual companions on the journey

My local church community
at St. James Episcopal Church, South Pasadena,
under the spiritual leadership of the
Reverend Canon Anne Tumilty, my beloved Rector

San Fernando Valley Oblate Group
(Saint Andrew's Abbey, Valyermo, CA), my Oblate community
hosted by Ron and Jody Berges, with whom
I have journeyed for three years now

Ignatian Guys Group—2010–2011
(Rick, Jimmy, Os, JR, Daniel, and Liam), for sticking it out
together through thick and thin for nine long months
doing the Spiritual Exercises of St. Ignatius

Spiritual Direction Monthly Peer Supervision Group
(Diane, Jeanne, Christy, and Madeline), for our sacred times of
learning together, via verbatim presentations and consultations

The Society of Urban Monks
(www.urban-monk.org), headed by Joe Colletti and Sofia Herrera

The Henri Nouwen Society
(www.henrinouwen.org), for their partnership and all-out support

Finally, my new colleagues
in the Master of Arts in Spiritual Formation and
Leadership (MSFL) Online Program under the
Department of Theology at Spring Arbor University, Michigan,
for warmly welcoming me to the Spring Arbor community

About the Author

Wil Hernandez was born and raised in the Philippines. Prior to coming to the United States in 1995 to pursue his Master of Theology degree (ThM, Counseling Ministry major), he worked full-time with an international, interdenominational Christian parachurch organization for eighteen years. Wil finished his PhD in Practical Theology with a concentration in spirituality in 2005 at Fuller Theological Seminary, with additional summer studies at the University of Notre Dame and Loyola Marymount University.

A trained counselor and a certified spiritual director, Wil devotes part of his time "companioning" others in their spiritual journey, aside from teaching courses on the spirituality of Henri Nouwen at various Catholic and Protestant seminaries and universities including Fuller Theological Seminary, Azusa Pacific University, Loyola Marymount University, Hope International University, Oblate School of Theology (Texas), Tyndale Seminary (Toronto), and Spring Arbor University (Michigan). Wil regularly conducts retreats, workshops, seminars, and lectures across the United States and abroad focusing on Henri Nouwen. He authored *Henri Nouwen: A Spirituality of Imperfection* (2006) and *Henri Nouwen and Soul Care: A Ministry of Integration* (2008), both published by Paulist Press.

Currently, Wil holds the E. A. and Bessie Andrews Endowed Chair in Spiritual Formation at Spring Arbor University where he teaches as an associate professor of Christian spirituality and directs its online Master of Arts in Spiritual Formation and Leadership (MFSL) program. He remains associated with The Leadership Institute as affiliate staff.

Wil has been married to Juliet for more than twenty-five years and together with their two adult sons, Jonathan and David, they make their home in Arcadia, California. Wil attends St. James Episcopal Church in South Pasadena.

For more information

about the Henri Nouwen courses,

retreats, seminars, and workshops

that Wil Hernandez regularly conducts,

please visit

www.nouwenlegacy.com

or email Wil at

wil@nouwenlegacy.com

green press
INITIATIVE

Paulist Press is committed to preserving ancient forests and natural resources. We elected to print this title on 30% post consumer recycled paper, processed chlorine free. As a result, for this printing, we have saved:

4 Trees (40' tall and 6-8" diameter)
1 Million BTUs of Total Energy
420 Pounds of Greenhouse Gases
1,895 Gallons of Wastewater
120 Pounds of Solid Waste

Paulist Press made this paper choice because our printer, Thomson-Shore, Inc., is a member of Green Press Initiative, a nonprofit program dedicated to supporting authors, publishers, and suppliers in their efforts to reduce their use of fiber obtained from endangered forests.

For more information, visit www.greenpressinitiative.org

Environmental impact estimates were made using the Environmental Defense Paper Calculator. For more information visit: www.papercalculator.org.